NACHTIGALL

The Ukrainian Battalion in the Wehrmacht (1941)

Recollections and Reflections of the Last Surviving Member

MYROSLAW KALBA

Translated by J. M. Berezowsky

DEDICATION

I dedicate this book to the memory of my comrades-in-arms who served in the Nachtigall Battalion and in the Ukrainian Insurgent Army. They were supported by countless and often nameless patriots who sacrificed their lives so that Ukraine, along with other nations, might attain freedom.

Myroslaw Kalba

TABLE OF CONTENTS

v

PART THREE

THE UKRAINIAN BATTALION NACHTIGALL
An Historical Perspective

In early 1941, war between Nazi Germany and Soviet Russia appeared imminent. The leadership of the Organization of Ukrainian Nationalists led by Stepan Bandera (OUN-B)) concluded that it was an opportune time for Ukrainians to take advantage of the conflict between Germany and Russia. To further Ukrainian aspirations for freedom and independence, the OUN-B was determined to obtain military training for several hundred of its members. They would constitute the officer core of a future Ukrainian army.

OUN-B member Riko Yaryi was authorized by the leadership of the organization to begin negotiations with representatives of the High Command of the Wehrmacht, the German Army. A citizen of the Third Reich since Austria's Anschluss with Germany, Riko Yaryi had served in the Ukrainian Galician Army in 1918, where he had developed friendships with various German officers. His negotiations were conducted with German army reserve officers and were finalized in April 1941. The secret agreement was approved by senior officers of the Wehrmacht High Command and by Admiral Canaris, head of Germany's military intelligence. It provided for the military training of 600-800 members of the OUN-B by the Wehrmacht. The men would be under the military command of the Wehrmacht in the field, but would remain under the "political" supervision of Ukrainian officers selected by the OUN-B.

Hitler's racist policies precluded the open training and arming of so many Ukrainians. The only way to do so, therefore, was to utilize an existing military formation, a unit already being trained for special actions, the Brandenburg Corps d.o.d. 800. Since this unit was subordinated to the Amt. Ausland/Abwehr (German military intelligence) it would be immune from Nazi political interference.

Officers of the Brandenburg Corps were assigned to train the Ukrainian volunteers, who were formed into two battalions. One battalion was organized in Austria and was given the code name Roland. The second battalion was organized in the area administered by the General Government (Poland proper and the western Ukrainian territories) and was given the code name Nachtigall. The political commander of the Nachtigall Battalion was Roman Shukhevych, who would later become the Supreme Commander of the Ukrainian Insurgent Army (Ukrayinska Povstanska Armiya – UPA).

The Nachtigall Battalion began its basic training in April 1941 at the Wehrmacht's large training camp in Neuhammer, Silesia. The training lasted approximately six weeks. It did not include specialized training in espionage, subversive activities, or training in parachuting, as has often been alleged by some propagandists.

Toward the end of May 1941, the German High Command of the 17th Army issued the following secret order (German Federal Archives RH 20-17/276):

> Armeeoberkommando 17
> A. H. Qu., den 29.5.41
> Abt. Ia/Ic, Nr 282/41 g. Kdos GEHEIM
> Concerning: Addition of one battalion to Brandenburg Corps D.o.D. 800
> Group of the Southern armies
> It is requested that command be accepted of a sufficiently large unit to the 1st Battalion of Brandenburg Corps d.o.d. 800 and a separate formation (Sonderformation) Nachtigall.

The places where it is expected to be engaged are:
> a). Lviv and its environs, with the goal of securing the roads, business enterprises, and infrastructure (railway lines, water supply, factories, post offices, and radio stations).

b).The bridge near Peremyshl. It is expected that only one unit will be engaged, provided that heavier military action is not necessary to secure the bridge. c). In the course of operations, it may be necessary to drop sabotage subunits beyond the front lines for the destruction of bridges across the Dniester river. It is, therefore, requested that the battalion be supplemented by at least 60 parachutists.

For the High Command
Chief of the General Staff, Lt. Colonel Mueller

This document establishes several important points: 1). The Nachtigall Battalion was a separate part of the German Army, without a designation; 2). The Battalion did not belong to the Brandenburg Corps d.o.d. 800 for special assignments, but was simply subordinated to it militarily; 3). The Nachtigall Battalion's goals were very precisely and clearly specified in the order and had nothing to do with potential police actions or other interaction with the civilian population.

On June 18, 1941, shortly before the German attack on the Soviet Union, the Nachtigall Battalion was moved toward the Soviet border. At that time, command of the Battalion was assumed by the commander of the First Battalion of the Brandenburg Corps d.o.d. 800. During the night of June 22-23, the Nachtigall Battalion crossed the border near the town of Peremyshl and began advancing toward Lviv, which it reached in the early morning hours of June 30. In accordance with its orders, the Battalion occupied a number of strategic objectives in the city, including the radio station. The Battalion was relieved of this assignment by German troops within the next day or two.

On July 6 or 7 the Battalion was ordered to leave Lviv with Brandenburg Corps d.o.d. 800, and advance eastward to Vinnytsya, via Ternopil and Proskuriv. After the taking of Vinnytsya, the Battalion was given a furlough and remained in the town of Yuzvyn. There, its members learned that the top leadership of the OUN-B had been arrested by the Gestapo. In protest, the members of the Nachtigall Battalion unanimously refused further cooperation with the German Army and were soon disarmed by the Germans. The officers and men of the now disarmed and formally disbanded Battalion were transported back to Neuhammer for additional training, and waited for the German authority's decision concerning their fate.

In October, the members of the Nachtigall and Roland Battalions were reorganized into Schutzmannschaftsbattalion-201, a police-security formation employed to protect roads and bridges in the German-occupied territories of the Soviet Union. Coerced into signing individual contracts to serve one year in this new battalion, they were sent to serve in Belarus until December 1942 when their contracts expired. Unanimously refusing to renew their contract, the men were disarmed and returned to Ukraine on January 6, 1943.

With the possible exception of some Ukrainians, few people seemed interested in the Nachtigall Battalion after the war. In 1959, however, a sudden change occurred. At a press conference held in East Berlin on October 23, 1959, East German professor Albert Norden accused West German federal minister Theodor Oberlander of having committed war crimes during World War II. Norden alleged that Oberlander, who had been the German Abwehr's liaison officer with the Nachtigall Battalion, had ordered the Battalion to arrest and eliminate a group of prominent Polish academics in the city of Lviv while the Battalion was deployed there. Norden further alleged that the Nachtigall Battalion had not only murdered the Polish academics, but had also murdered some 3,000 Jewish residents of the city.

Theodor Oberlander, appointed Minister for Refugees, Repatriates and War Victims in 1953 by West German Chancellor Konrad Adenauer, had incurred the wrath of the Soviets and East Germans for his anti-communist views and policies. To embarrass the West

German Government and pressure Chancellor Adenauer into dismissing Oberlander, the Soviets accused him, using Norden, of Nazi war crimes. Reviewing his dossier, the Soviets had discovered that in June-July of 1941 Oberlander had been the Abwehr's contact officer with the Nachtigall Battalion. Thus was born the idea of getting rid of the detested West German minister and striking a blow against Ukrainian nationalists at the same time. The Soviets quickly produced several "witnesses" and the matter soon gained international attention. The well-organized Soviet campaign, aided by subservient Communist Parties in the West, eventually did result in Oberlander's resignation. However, a West German judicially ordered prosecutorial inquiry found no credible evidence to support the accusations which the communists had made against Oberlander and the Nachtigall Battalion.

Reliable witnesses and objective Polish authors have disproved the Soviet accusations made against the Nachtigall Battalion (see *Przeglad-Lekarski*, XX, Seria II, nl, Krakow, 1964; Albert Zigmunt; *Lwowski Wydzial Lekarski w Czasie Okupacji Hitleriwskiej*, 1941-1944, Wroclaw, 1975). One may also consult official Soviet documents from before and after the "Oberlander Affair." They appear in several publications and include: 1). Excerpts from the "Official investigation concerning crimes of the Fascist occupiers of Lviv", compiled by the Regional Committee of the Verkhovna Rada of the Ukrainian SSR, found in *Soviet Ukraine in the Years of the Great Patriotic War, 1941-45*, Kiev, 1963, pp. 274-281; and 2). Report of the Special Commission investigating these crimes on the territory of Lviv Oblast, found in *The German-Fascist Occupation Regime in Ukraine*, Kiev, 1963, pp. 349-351. Neither of these publications made any accusations against the Nachtigall Battalion. Nor did any accusations of alleged war crimes appear in more recent publications, for instance: *Istoriya Zasterihaye* (History Forewarns), Kiev, 1986, and in *Nazi Crimes in Ukraine, 1941-1944*, Kiev, 1987.

Nevertheless, the Soviet campaign against Oberlander and the Nachtigall Battalion beginning in 1959 achieved some of its intended goals. Believing the Soviet assertions, French author Henri Michel in his book *La Deuxieme Guerre Mondial*, Paris, 1968, p. 265, wrote: "All occupied territories were transformed into a theatre of previously planned exterminations. Many examples were described during the Nuremberg Trial. The Gestapo had prepared lists of individuals condemned to death in advance. A special battalion, named Nachtigall, belonging to the Brandenburg regiment, carried out the executions."

German war documents have clearly established, however, that the 1st Battalion of the Brandenburg Corps d.o.d. 800 and the Nachtigall Battalion were involved only in seizing and occupying important physical objectives, warehouses, and institutions in Lviv. Executions of civilians were conducted by the German security police and the SD, which arrived in Lviv on June 30, 1941. The Nachtigall Battalion never participated in any police action, or in the execution of civilians. Its name never came up during the Nuremberg Trial. Expressly relying on the conclusions of the Soviet Extraordinary Commission for the Investigation of German Crimes in the City and Region of Lviv (document NO USSR-6/1), the international tribunal at Nuremberg, during its February 15, 1946 session, concluded that the executions were the work of special groups of the Gestapo and SD (IMT, Germsession on an publication, volume 7, P.540-541).

On August 30, 1946 at the Nuremberg proceedings, the Soviet General Prosecutor, Rudenko, made the following statement:

> The intelligentsia also became an object of repression by the Gestapo…These acts of repression were conducted pursuant to preexisting plans. Thus, for example, units of the Gestapo already had a list of prominent members of the city's intelligentsia who were to be executed. Mass arrests and executions of professors, doctors, lawyers, writers, and artists began immediately upon the seizure of Lviv by the German Army. The

investigation, conducted after the liberation of Lviv by the Red Army, determined that the Germans murdered 70 scientists, artists, and engineers, whose bodies were burned by the Gestapo. (IMT, XXIII, P. 394)

In Soviet and communist Polish publications on this subject prior to October 1959, no accusations were ever leveled against the Nachtigall Battalion. See, for example, Tadeusz Cyprian and Jerzy Sawicki: *Nie Oszczedzac Polski*. Warszawa, 1959; and an English-language book titled: *Nazi Rule in Poland, 1939-1945*, Warsaw, 1961.

Notwithstanding the actual historical facts, however, the Nachtigall Battalion became a convenient target for the Soviets when they launched their campaign against a West German government minister whom they were determined to punish for his anti-Soviet views and policies.

Volodymyr Kosyk
Professor of History
Sorbonne, Paris
Ukrainian Free University, Munich

PREFACE

Seven decades ago, in April 1941, two army battalions composed of some 660 Ukrainian volunteers were formed to participate in the upcoming invasion of the Soviet Union that was being planned by Germany. The battalions were placed under the military command of the Wehrmacht, the German Army, and code-named Nachtigall and Roland. Together, they opened a significant new chapter in the history of Ukraine's long struggle for freedom and independence.

The men of the Nachtigall and Roland Battalions, while cooperating with and forming a part of the German armed forces, never swore allegiance to the Third Reich or to its Fuhrer, Adolf Hitler. Their allegiance belonged to a future Ukrainian State and to the Organization of Ukrainian Nationalists (OUN). The goal of the OUN - a disciplined, clandestine, revolutionary organization founded in 1929 - was the creation of a free and independent Ukrainian State. Its members and leadership believed that the impending conflict between Nazi Germany and Soviet Russia presented Ukrainians with an opportunity to secure their nation's independence. For that reason, they were eager to participate in the conflict.

June 30, 1941, one week after entering Soviet-held Ukrainian territory with the German Army, the 330 men of the Nachtigall Battalion marched into the city of Lviv. They immediately declared their support for the independent Ukrainian State proclaimed that very day at the headquarters of Prosvita (Enlightenment Society). The Battalion's members pledged their allegiance and reaffirmed their loyalty to the newly-formed provisional Ukrainian Government, headed by Premier Yaroslav Stetsko, and to the leadership of the OUN-B, headed by Stepan Bandera.

It became clear almost immediately that the Nazi regime would not tolerate a sovereign, independent Ukrainian State nor a Ukrainian Government. When the Gestapo began arresting members of the Provisional Ukrainian Government and members of the OUN-B leadership in early July 1941, the Nachtigall and Roland Battalions immediately terminated their cooperation with the German Army. By doing so, the members of both Battalions exposed themselves to the possibility of severe punishment, possibly even execution, at the hands of the German military or political authorities.

Relatively little was known about the Nachtigall and Roland Battalions until recently, even in Ukraine. The Soviet regime stifled any open discussion of Ukraine's long struggle for independence. The Soviets worked continuously to besmirch the heroic deeds of the tens of thousands of courageous men and women who had been engaged in Ukraine's struggle for freedom during the 20th century. Following the Kremlin's instructions, the communist regimes in Poland and East Germany willingly participated in Soviet efforts to portray the Ukrainian independence movement and its members in the darkest possible light. Even today, one can still find books, magazine articles, and postings on the Internet disparaging Ukraine's struggle for independence, particularly during the Second World War. Ukrainian patriots and nationalists are often portrayed simplistically and maliciously as fascists, Nazi collaborators, and anti-Semites. These false and misleading portrayals of Ukrainians essentially reiterate, word-for-word, the false accusations disseminated years ago by various Soviet government spokesmen, hack writers, *faux* journalists and "scholars." These spurious allegations remain as untrue today as they were when first made.

In the following pages the reader will learn about the actual activities of the Nachtigall Battalion. I was a member of the Battalion from its inception in April 1941, to its disbandment in October of that year. I will respond to the spurious accusations which have been leveled against the Battalion and its members concerning the tragic events which occurred in the city of Lviv during the first days of July 1941. I have included excerpts from the personal recollections of several German Army officers and from several of my comrades in the Battalion. I will also describe my subsequent service in Schutzmannshaftsbattalion-201, a police-security battalion deployed in Belarus during 1942. Members of the Nachtigall and Roland Battalions had been coerced into joining this formation after the disbandment of their two battalions.

I am extremely gratified that my previous books about the Nachtigall Battalion, published in Ukrainian and Polish, have found an interested and receptive readership. As the last surviving member of the Nachtigall Battalion, I feel that I owe a sacred duty to the memory of my departed comrades-in-arms to accurately and truthfully tell their story. It is equally my sacred duty to respond to the spurious and malicious allegations made against the Battalion in which my comrades and I served. By publishing my recollections and reflections in English, I hope to enable a much wider circle of readers and students of modern history to learn the truth about the Nachtigall Battalion and its positive role in the struggle of the people of Ukraine for their freedom and independence.

This book is published on the 70th anniversary of the founding of the Ukrainian Insurgent Army *(Ukrayinska Povstanska Armiya - UPA)*, which continued the noble struggle for Ukrainian freedom and independence well into the early 1950s. Its officer core consisted of many men, including myself, who had previously been members of the Nachtigall Battalion.

Myroslaw Kalba
November 2012

ACKNOWLEDGEMENT

My most sincere thanks to J. M. Berezowsky, the translator, and others who assisted him in editing and translating my manuscript, and preparing this book for publication: Lydia Taraschuk, Marta Kwitkowsky, Adrian Kwitkowsky, Larissa Babak, Zhdan Lassovsky, Leo Iwaskiw, and Vera Kalba. Their combined efforts have made possible this publication of my recollections concerning the Nachtigall Battalion, and my personal reflections regarding the important historical role of the Battalion and refutation of the false allegations made against its members.

Myroslaw Kalba
November 2012

CHRONOLOGY OF THE NACHTIGALL BATTALION
(1941)

Early April	Recruitment of members begins in Krakow, Poland.
Early May	Members begin basic training in Neuhammer, Silesia.
June 17	Battalion members complete basic training.
June 18	Battalion leaves Neuhammer for German-Soviet border.
June 22	Battalion crosses the Buh River and enters Soviet-occupied Ukraine.
June 30	Battalion enters the city of Lviv at 4:30 a.m. and occupies strategic locations.
July 1	Battalion is relieved by German units.
July 1-6	Battalion members receive a one-week furlough and remain in the city.
July 7	Battalion leaves Lviv with the Brandenburg d.o.d. 800 Corps.
July 14	Battalion enters the city of Vinnytsya and begins a weeklong furlough.
July 15	Battalion refuses further cooperation with the German Army and is placed in custody.
August 13	Battalion is ordered back to Neuhammer and its members are interned.

October 19   Members of Battalion arrive in Frankfurt-an-der-Oder.

October 21   Roland Battalion arrives in Frankfurt-an-der-Oder.

Late October Members of both battalions combined into one *Schutzmannshaftsbattalion-201*.

CHRONOLOGY OF
SCHUTZMANNSHAFTSBATTALION-201 (1941-42)

Late October	New Battalion begins period of retraining and awaits deployment.
March 23, 1942	Battalion arrives in Belarus, and begins its assignment of guarding roads, bridges, and searching for and eliminating Soviet partisans.
Late December	Battalion members unanimously refuse to renew their service contract.
January 6, 1943	Battalion is officially disbanded in Mogilev, Belarus.
Mid-January, 1943	Members of Battalion leave Belarus for Kyiv, Ukraine.

FROM THE TRANSLATOR

This book is an edited translation of Myroslaw Kalba's manuscript entitled *V Oboroni Zneslavlennya DUN* (*Responding to the Defamation of DUN*), which recounts his membership and activities in the Nachtigall Battalion in 1941, and responds to various allegations which have been made against it. The author was the last surviving member of the Nachtigall Battalion.

The Nachtigall Battalion was a unit comprised of some 330 Ukrainian volunteers under the military command of the Wehrmacht, the German Army, which advanced into Soviet-occupied Ukraine on June 22, 1941, at the start of the Soviet-German war. The acronym DUN stands for Druzhyny Ukrayinskykh Natsionalistiv (Legion of Ukrainian Nationalists). DUN was a group of approximately six hundred and sixty young men who served with the German Army in 1941. Most of the men in the Legion were members of the Organization of Ukrainian Nationalists led by Stepan Bandera (OUN-B). The Legion of Ukrainian Nationalists (DUN) was divided into two battalions, Nachtigall and Roland, each numbering about 330 men. The units were organized by the OUN-B and trained by the German Wehrmacht, which maintained military command of the battalions. The author's experiences in the Nachtigall Battalion and its successor unit, Schutzmannschaftsbattalion-201, are the subject of this book.

As translator of Myroslaw Kalba's manuscript, I believe it is important to make a few introductory remarks.

The defeat of Nazi Germany was unquestionably a welcome victory over a truly evil regime and ideology. However, the objective reader should also realize that the defeat of Nazi Germany left intact an equally malevolent regime: Stalinist Russia. The defeat of Germany not only helped Soviet Russia maintain its despotic hold over nations like Ukraine and Belarus (which the Bolsheviks had conquered shortly after the First World War) but allowed it to extend its rule over nations which had been independent before the war. These included Bulgaria, Czechoslovakia, East Germany, Estonia, Hungary, Latvia, Lithuania, Poland, and Romania.

Hundreds of thousands of American soldiers, sailors, and pilots sacrificed their lives to defeat Nazi Germany, and American tax dollars largely financed the Allied war effort. Unfortunately, most Americans remained unaware of the difficult circumstances in which countries like Ukraine found themselves under Stalinist oppression. Ukrainians and other victims of Soviet aggression (Belarus, Estonia, Latvia and Lithuania) viewed the upcoming struggle between Soviet Russia and Nazi Germany from a very different perspective. They saw the struggle between Germany and Stalinist Russia as a possible, realistic opportunity to restore their nations' freedom and independence.

During the Second World War, Americans were influenced by the federal government and the media to think of the Soviet Union as a friendly ally. The American press often referred amiably to Josef Stalin, the Soviet dictator, as "Uncle Joe", notwithstanding the fact (known to many in the U. S. government and media) that he was a brutal tyrant and a mass-murderer. "Uncle Joe" was responsible for the deaths of millions of people in his own country and had, in fact, been Hitler's willing ally.

In 1918, Ukrainians declared their nation's independence after two-and-a-half centuries of despotic Russian tsarist rule. During those years, Ukraine's churches, schools, cultural, educational, and political institutions had been either completely destroyed or thoroughly russified. Since the early 1700s, the Russian government had repeatedly issued various edicts, orders, and instructions severely limiting and even prohibiting the use of the Ukrainian language. The infamous Ems Ukaz, forbidding the publication of books, newspapers, and magazines in the Ukrainian language, was signed in 1876 by Tsar Alexander II in the German resort town of Bad Ems. After their victory in the October Revolution of 1917, the new Communist rulers of Russia, just like their tsarist predecessors, vehemently opposed Ukrainian independence, and by 1921, effectively reasserted Russian control over most of central and eastern Ukraine.

Between 1918 and the outbreak of World War II, Ukraine and other nations lost tens of thousands of their compatriots to the murderous firing squads of the CHEKA, OGPU, and NKVD. Hundreds of thousands of Ukrainian farmers died of starvation during the years 1920-21 after Lenin repeatedly ordered massive confiscations of grain from Ukraine's farmers in order to feed the Red Army. Millions of Ukrainians, Russians, Poles, Jews, and members of other nations were imprisoned or exiled to the far reaches of Northern Russia or Siberia. Most of them were worked to death in the labor camps of the Soviet GULAG. It is tragically ironic that the rapid industrialization of the Soviet Union, which so impressed many in the United States during the Depression years of the 1930s, was largely the product of slave labor performed by massive numbers of political prisoners, many of whom perished from exhaustion or hunger.

At the beginning of the 1930s, countless hardworking, independent Ukrainian farmers were derisively labeled "blood-sucking kulaks" by the Soviet authorities, forcibly thrown off their farms, and exiled to distant parts of the Soviet Union, together with their families. Several million Ukrainian farmers perished from starvation during the genocidal famine (Holodomor) of 1932-33, caused by the merciless confiscation of their harvests and foodstuffs by the Soviet government as punishment for their reluctance to join government-run collective farms. Special laws were enacted to punish anyone, including children, who dared to scavenge the farm fields for grain which might be left in the fields after the harvest. A system of internal passports was introduced for the specific purpose of keeping the starving farmers from leaving their villages to seek food or work elsewhere, and city dwellers were forbidden to give any food or assistance to the few villagers who managed to make it to the city. Any public mention of the famine was prohibited and harshly punished. Reports of the famine, which appeared in the Western press, were routinely dismissed by the Soviets and their sympathizers as "malicious fascist propaganda."

Beginning in 1930, the Soviets resumed arresting, imprisoning, exiling, and executing thousands of Ukrainian intellectuals, including actors, artists, educators, journalists, poets, scholars, writers, and church and community leaders. The brief and relatively benign period of "Ukrainianization" during the 1920s was brought to a screeching halt and almost overnight, Russian became the required language in Ukrainian schools, colleges and universities, and in the media. All Ukrainian cultural and educational institutions were either closed or changed to the point of becoming unrecognizable. Not a single Ukrainian Orthodox church was allowed to remain open, and all Ukrainian Orthodox believers, whose bishops were imprisoned, were forced to join the Russian Orthodox Church. This hellish period of terror and mass murder in Ukraine was largely ignored by Western governments and the press. The governments of Great Britain, France, and the United States were focused on their own economic troubles and the threat of instability in Western Europe; the tragic events occurring in Ukraine were simply not in their "field of vision."

Is it any wonder then, that many in Ukraine and in other East European nations were encouraged by Nazi Germany's antagonism toward Soviet Russia? They saw in Germany a potential ally who might help them in their fight for freedom and independence. In the initial months of the Soviet-German conflict, hundreds of thousands of Ukrainian soldiers, who were conscripted into the Red Army, demonstrated their unwillingness to fight for the Soviet regime and surrendered *en masse* to the Germans. Many Ukrainians openly welcomed the invading German soldiers, seeing in them potential liberators from Stalinist oppression. Similarly, the young volunteers who signed up for military duty with the German Army in 1941 as members of the Nachtigall Battalion also believed that they might help their country, Ukraine, win its independence from Soviet Russia.

The second part of Myroslaw Kalba's book deals with the various accusations made against the Nachtigall Battalion, and against Ukrainian nationalists in general. The author reminds us that practically from the very first day it seized power, the Soviet Government engaged in the continuous denigration and defamation of Ukrainian and other "nationalisms" (except, curiously, Russian nationalism). The Bolsheviks, as the Russian Communists then called themselves, made effective use of force, terror, propaganda, disinformation and falsehood, to combat, neutralize or physically destroy any "bourgeois nationalist" who dared to aspire to independence for his or her country.

The Soviets also maintained a closely-controlled judiciary which was totally subservient to the Communist Party and the Soviet State. It is for this reason, the author argues persuasively, that any documentary or physical evidence and testimony of witnesses produced by the Soviets was inherently suspect and unworthy of belief in a court of law. Documents and physical evidence were often doctored or fabricated. Purported witnesses invariably were coached by their NKVD/KGB handlers. They were ominously reminded of their "duty to the Socialist Motherland" or threatened with reprisal if they refused to testify as directed by the authorities. The author points out that in all totalitarian states, like Soviet Russia, the courts have always been employed by the regime to maintain its authority and control, and that truth and justice have been alien concepts to the judiciary of Soviet Russia and other communist countries. The decisions of the judges were invariably predetermined from the moment that charges were brought against an individual, and the accused could never expect or get a fair trial.

Hopefully, these introductory comments will help the reader better understand the relevant historical background and the political circumstances which existed during the brief period of time which the author discusses in this book. In the course of preparing the English translation, I have benefited greatly from the numerous comments and suggestions made by Lydia Taraschuk and Marta Kwitkowsky.

This book, written by an actual participant in the events described, should be a useful addition to the literature concerning the history and politics of the Second World War. It also will give the reader an appreciation of the courage, commitment, and personal sacrifice made by many thousands of Ukrainian patriots who fought for their nation's freedom and independence during that war.

The names of various individuals and organizations relevant to the text, and various terms which may be unfamiliar to the general reader, are listed and explained briefly in the Glossary. Slavic words and names have been transliterated to approximate their phonetic sound in the original language.

J. M. Berezowsky
Translator

INTRODUCTION

As the Russian and Austro-Hungarian Empires disintegrated toward the end of World War I many nations, that had been their unwilling subjects, began to assert their independence. Poland, partitioned by its neighbors in 1798, resumed its existence as an independent state in 1918. Ukraine also declared its independence in January 1918. Unfortunately, its heroic efforts to maintain this independence were unsuccessful. Soviet troops promptly invaded Ukraine and defeated the poorly armed troops of the Ukrainian National Republic. Ukrainian lands were divided among Soviet Russia, Poland, Czechoslovakia, and Romania.

Ukrainians in western Ukraine proclaimed an independent state, the Western Ukrainian National Republic, in the city of Lviv on November 1, 1918. Soon, however, it fell to superior Polish forces, which had been provided with arms and ammunition by the French Government. In 1923, the Conference of Ambassadors, which had been established by the victorious Entente to implement the terms of the Versailles Peace Treaty, awarded the Ukrainian ethnic territories of eastern Galicia and Volhynia to Poland. An express proviso stated that the Ukrainian territories be granted political and cultural autonomy, and a referendum about the future status of the Ukrainian lands was to be held within a reasonable time. While the Polish Government readily accepted the Ukrainian territories awarded to it by the Conference, it never honored its obligation to grant Ukrainians autonomy and never held a referendum. Instead, the Polish government essentially turned the Ukrainian ethnic territories into a Polish colony and severely curtailed the civil, cultural, and political rights of the Ukrainian inhabitants of eastern Galicia and Volhynia.

Ukrainians of eastern Galicia had enjoyed substantial cultural and political rights under the Austrian Hapsburg monarchy. They had their own schools, an active intelligentsia, and an experienced cadre of civil servants. Under the new Polish administration, however, they were soon deprived of many of the rights which they had enjoyed under the Austrians. Ukrainians were barred from important positions in government, the police, and army. The Ukrainian school system was all but destroyed. During Austrian rule the Lemberg *curatoria* had more than 2400 schools where the language of instruction was Ukrainian. By 1934, under Polish rule, only 457 schools remained with Ukrainian as the language of instruction, and the majority of them provided instruction only through grade 4. In Volhynia, the number of Ukrainian schools went from about 500 down to only six in 1934.

Polish authorities began resettling large numbers of Poles into Volhynia and initiated a brutal campaign of "pacification" against the Ukrainian population in the territories they administered. This campaign involved the widespread destruction of Ukrainian churches, schools, libraries, and cultural institutions. It even included severe physical beatings of peaceful civilians. The "pacification" program was brutally implemented by units of the Polish police and army. Quoting Polish author Zbigniew Okon: "Marshall Pilsudski employed harsher measures against Ukrainians than Hitler was to employ against the Poles in 1939". (ANEKS 5-6 VII, 1998). Polish police authorities imprisoned hundreds of Ukrainian political activists at the Bereza Kartuska concentration camp, many without being formally charged or tried in a court of law.

The draconian, anti-Ukrainian policies of the Polish Government inevitably led to the emergence of a radicalized resistance movement, especially among the Ukrainian youth of eastern Galicia and Volhynia. (See ANEKS, above). At the forefront of that movement was the OUN, a clandestine organization founded in 1929 by surviving members of the ill-fated independence movement of the early 1920s. The radicalized younger members of the OUN were no longer willing to accept second-class Polish citizenship and continued cultural and political oppression by the Polish government. They were ready and eager to participate in a "war of national liberation" against the Polish authorities and against the Soviets, who occupied Central and Eastern Ukraine. Many of those young OUN members eagerly volunteered for the Nachtigall Battalion when the opportunity arose. I was one of them.

xxx

PART ONE

The Legion of Ukrainian Nationalists

The Second World War effectively began on September 1, 1939 with Germany's invasion of Poland. The German attack on Poland occurred with the explicit approval of the Soviets, who had concluded a peace treaty with Nazi Germany known as the Molotov-Ribbentrop Pact, just a few days earlier. Among other things, the pact allowed the Soviets to occupy and annex the Ukrainian territories of eastern Galicia and Volhynia, administered by Poland since the last war, and to incorporate the Baltic states of Lithuania, Latvia, and Estonia into the Soviet Union. In turn, the Soviets obligated themselves to provide Germany with large quantities of natural resources in order to enable Germany to prosecute its war in Western Europe.

The German Blitzkrieg, employing massive, coordinated tank and air attacks, very quickly defeated the inferior Polish forces. After defeating Poland and dividing its territory with Soviet Russia, Nazi Germany promptly attacked its western neighbors and quickly brought them to heel. Hitler suddenly found himself drawing the borders of a "New Europe," and soon it became clear that the partnership between Hitler and Stalin would not last much longer. As soon as Germany secured its conquests in western and southern Europe, it would attack Soviet Russia too. The "New Europe" envisioned by Hitler and the Nazis would simply not be possible without the defeat and subjugation of the Soviet Union.

Shortly after the German invasion of Poland and the contemporaneous Soviet occupation and annexation of eastern Galicia and Volhynia, the various Ukrainian political parties, allowed to function under Polish rule, were forcibly disbanded by the Soviets. The Soviets immediately established a one-party system and prohibited any political or cultural activities not sanctioned and fully controlled by them. They quickly inundated eastern Galicia and Volhynia with members of the NKVD, their secret police. They began arresting

3

thousands of Ukrainian cultural, community, and political leaders. Those patriotic Ukrainians, not imprisoned by the NKVD, decided to seize any opportunity which might present itself in order to free Ukraine from Soviet occupation.

It was then that Stepan Bandera, a charismatic young member of the OUN (the vanguard of the Ukrainian revolutionary movement) assumed leadership of a breakaway faction of the organization. This faction (designated in this book as OUN-B) included tens of thousands of deeply committed, idealistic members of the younger generation. They were convinced that freedom and independence could only be achieved by military force. They were willing to sacrifice their lives for the cause of Ukrainian independence.

Being in the midst of war, the Western powers were not interested in the "Ukrainian question" or in Ukrainian aspirations for independence. In 1918, the Western governments had voiced no protest when Bolshevik Russia overthrew the short-lived Ukrainian National Republic by military force. The West quietly stood by as the Communists imposed a reign of terror in Ukraine and starved millions of its farmers to death in 1921 and again in the early 1930s. Their reaction was no different when the Polish government reneged on its promises to give Ukrainians in eastern Galicia and Volhynia self-rule. Now, in the early 1940s, the West was responding in the same way: it showed no concern for the political and cultural oppression of Ukraine by the Soviets and indicated no support for the rights and legitimate aspirations of Ukrainians. The West was interested primarily in defeating the Nazis and restoring the political situation to the *status quo ante*, in which there was no place for an independent Ukraine.

The new generation of Ukrainians, led by the OUN-B, seized the initiative and committed itself wholeheartedly to the continuing struggle for Ukrainian independence by any means possible. Russia, whatever its professed ideology at any given time, had always vehemently opposed Ukrainian independence and used every tool at its disposal, to thwart Ukrainian aspirations for independent statehood. Ukrainian nationalists were therefore

4

determined to take advantage of the impending military conflict between Nazi Germany and Soviet Russia in pursuit of their goal: Ukrainian independence. They believed that once the German Army advanced ever deeper into the Soviet Union, the "Ukrainian question" would assume paramount importance, and circumstances would favor the Ukrainian cause. Ukrainian nationalists hoped that the current German leadership would not repeat the mistakes made by their predecessors during the First World War. They hoped, perhaps naively, that this time the Germans would realize that they simply could not defeat, occupy, and govern the vast territories of the Soviet Union without the assistance and cooperation of Ukrainians and other nations subjugated by the Soviets.

Ukrainian nationalists certainly had no reason to put blind trust in the Nazis. Some of them had undoubtedly read Hitler's *Mein Kampf*, in which he made no secret of his racist scorn for Slavs, and of his intention to seize the bountiful fields of Ukraine as a "breadbasket" for Germans. Ukrainians, like all other Untermenschen (inferior or subhuman nations), would simply become slave laborers, whose sole purpose in life would be to serve, work for, and feed the German "Master Race." Hitler's recent "gift" of Carpatho-Ukraine to his Hungarian allies was still fresh in the minds of Galicia's and Volhynia's Ukrainians. They were even more resentful of his recent acquiescence to the Soviet occupation and annexation of eastern Galicia and Volhynia.

The OUN-B published a manifesto in 1940, proclaiming that the OUN-B was fighting "...for the freedom of nations and the freedom of the individual." The manifesto declared that Ukrainian independence could be achieved only by means of an armed struggle and the total defeat and complete dismemberment of the Soviet Union. In the spring of 1941, the Second Congress of the OUN-B adopted a Military Resolution which declared that "...the OUN must organize and train its own military forces, in order to accomplish its goals." The responsibility for implementing the objectives set forth in the Military Resolution was given to the organization's military leadership, headed by

Roman Shukhevych. With the help of his staff, Shukhevych prepared plans for the creation and training of military units within the OUN-B. The military units would be called Druzhyny Ukrayinskykh Natsionalistiv, DUN, (Legion of Ukrainian Nationalists) and would be composed entirely of volunteers willing to sacrifice their lives for the cause of Ukrainian independence. As soon as Shukhevych's plans were approved by the Provid (Leadership) of the OUN-B, recruitment and training of the volunteer military force would begin.

The OUN-B's Agreement with the Abwehr

I have no personal knowledge of the details of the agreement reached between the OUN-B leadership and the Abwehr, the German Army's Intelligence Service. However, gleaned from my many discussions with my comrades and our conversations with our superior officers, I learned that the agreement provided for the recruitment and military training of several hundred Ukrainian volunteers. Our troops would serve on the Eastern Front under the military command of the Wehrmacht, but would constitute a distinctly Ukrainian military formation under the political command of our own officers, selected by the leadership of the OUN-B.

To the best of my knowledge, the following terms and conditions were agreed to by the OUN-B and the German Abwehr:

a. Recruitment of volunteers for the Legion would be conducted exclusively by the OUN-B. The OUN-B would retain political command of the Legion and be responsible for the ideological indoctrination of recruits, conducted in accordance with the OUN-B's ideology, political goals, and objectives.

b. The Legion would actively participate in the expected armed conflict against Soviet Russia and, eventually, provide military support for the government of an independent Ukrainian State, to be established in Kyiv.

c. The Legion would not be deployed against the Western Allies.

d. The Legion would have its own officers and chaplains and would serve under the Ukrainian flag. The Legion would swear allegiance to an

Independent Ukrainian State and to the leadership of the OUN-B, not to Germany nor its leadership. Members of the Legion would not be subjected to Nazi ideological indoctrination.

e. The Legion would receive military training from officers and non-commissioned officers of the German Army and would be under German command during military operations.

The highest officials in the German government and in the Nazi Party leadership, including Hitler, undoubtedly did not know about the agreement between the OUN-B and the Abwehr. The Abwehr included within its ranks individuals who appeared not to share the Nazis' crude racist attitudes towards the Slavic nations of Eastern Europe. Some of them seemed receptive to the idea of recognizing independent states on the territories which the Germans expected to take from the Soviets. Those states would, of course, be allied with Germany and would be expected to support its war effort. Alfred Rosenberg, the Nazi's "resident expert" on East European affairs, was also thought to be favorably inclined to the idea of recognizing an independent Ukraine in his personal vision of a "new Europe."

Adolf Hitler, Heinrich Himmler, Josef Goebbels, Hermann Goering, and Wehrmacht Generals Keitel and Jodl (the "Fuhrer's men" in the German Military High Command), on the other hand, remained steadfastly opposed to independence for any nation in Eastern Europe or in the territories which they expected to seize from Soviet Russia. They undoubtedly would have forbidden the military training of Ukrainians by the German Army had they been aware of the Abwehr's agreement with the OUN-B. I have every reason to believe that the Military Leadership of the OUN-B had no contact, agreement, or dealings of any kind with either the SS or the Reichsicherheitshauptant (State Security Office of the German Reich). To the best of my knowledge, the OUN-B leadership had conducted negotiations only with representatives of the Abwehr, Germany's military intelligence.

The OUN-B's immediate objective was to acquire and have at its disposal a small, well-trained military force which could form the basis of a future Ukrainian army in a sovereign Ukrainian State. These military units could also be used to form the core of a partisan-guerilla force to be deployed against the Germans, if necessary. Anticipating the likely probability of a negative German response to Ukrainian political aspirations, the military leadership of the OUN-B was prepared to deploy the Legion against the German forces as well as against the Soviets. The possibility of a military struggle against two fronts was foreseen; in fact, that is exactly what happened.

Anticipating a two-front scenario, the leadership of the OUN-B took immediate steps to eliminate, or at least minimize, Polish-Ukrainian tensions. When conflict between Ukrainian nationalists and the Germans inevitably arose, Ukrainians were prepared for it. Thanks in large measure to the bold strategic objectives set by their commander, Roman Shukhevych, the Legion of Ukrainian Nationalists became a significant asset in the hands of the OUN-B's political leadership. When the break in relations with the Germans did come, former members of the Nachtigall and Roland Battalions quickly proved themselves to be effective combatants against the Germans no less than against the Soviets. The OUN-B's decision to organize the Legion of Ukrainian Nationalists was, I'm convinced, a wise strategic, political, and military decision.

Roman Shukhevych, commander of the Nachtigall Battalion, would later prove himself to be a masterful tactician of partisan-guerilla warfare as the supreme commander of the Ukrainian Insurgent Army (Ukrayinska Povstanska Armiya) UPA. The UPA's brave struggle against the Soviet and German invaders and occupants of Ukraine was one of the most heroic periods in Ukraine's history. Formed in late 1942, the UPA fought effectively against both the regular German Army, special SS forces, and against the Red Army and Soviet partisans. The UPA was even able to continue its struggle against the Soviets and their Communist allies well into the early 1950s, long after the Second World War had ended. The foundation of the Ukrainian Insurgent

Army was laid in the spring of 1941, with the creation of the Legion of Ukrainian Nationalists. The objective of the Legion and its two Battalions, Nachtigall and Roland, was to enter Kyiv, the capital of Ukraine, and provide military support for an interim Ukrainian Government to be established upon the declaration of Ukrainian Independence by representatives of the OUN-B and its allied political groups. This interim government was to be composed of representatives from all liberated areas of Ukraine. Professor Alexander Bohomolets, the president of the Ukrainian Academy of Sciences in Kyiv, was slated to become the Premier. The proposed interim government would include representatives of the Ukrainian National Committee, which had been organized shortly before the outbreak of the war; OUN-B members from the central region of Ukraine ("Sak-Mohyla," Serhij Sherstiuk and Osyp Pozychanyuk); OUN-B members from Galicia (Myron "Orlyk" and Roman Shukhevych); and representatives from various other political groups which were not affiliated with the OUN-B, but shared the common goal of Ukrainian independence. OUN-B plans also provided for a separate political body, a regional administration for the Western regions of Ukraine. It was to be set up in Lviv under Yaroslav Stetsko, and eventually it would subordinate itself to the national government in Kyiv. The Nachtigall and Roland Battalions were to become the officer core of a new Ukrainian Army. Its soldiers would be recruited from among Ukrainian prisoners of war who, it was believed, would surrender to the advancing German Army rather than risk their lives to defend the oppressive Soviet regime. Unfortunately, the Ukrainian and other soldiers in the Red Army who surrendered in huge numbers were brutally mistreated by their German captors. They were physically abused, inadequately fed, poorly clothed, and deprived of shelter and essential medical treatment. Several million Soviet prisoners of war needlessly perished in German prisoner of war camps. Contrary to the hopes of the OUN-B, the thousands of Ukrainian prisoners of war were not provided arms by the Germans nor encouraged to join the war against the Soviets as members of a new Ukrainian "liberation army." In their arrogance, the Germans foolishly refused to take advantage of the opportunity which had been presented to them in the initial months of the war. Here was an available pool of hundreds of thousands of brave and courageous soldiers of many nationalities, including Ukrainians and Russians, who could have easily been motivated to fight against Stalinist Russia, had they only been treated decently, not as a species of sub-humans.

A few days before Germany's attack on the Soviet Union on June 22, 1941, the Nazi Government ordered the arrest of Stepan Bandera, leader of the OUN-B. The Germans did so to prevent his return to Ukraine. Contemporaneously, the Gestapo summoned members of the Ukrainian National Committee in Krakow and intimidated them into withholding any support to those Ukrainians who might attempt to declare Ukrainian independence.

Military events quickly took a far different course than the Germans or the Ukrainian nationalists had expected. Making historically rapid progress in the days immediately following its June 22 attack on the Soviet Union, the German Army soon found itself unable to maintain its initial, astoundingly rapid pace. Its eastward advance slowed considerably, and it soon became increasingly obvious that the expected German occupation of Kyiv, the capital of Ukraine, would not occur as early as had been expected. This led the OUN-B leadership to move up the date on which to declare Ukrainian independence. The declaration would be announced in Lviv, the capital city of western Ukraine, where an interim Ukrainian government would be established. This government would subordinate itself to the national Ukrainian Government to be formed in Kyiv at a later time, once that city was reached by Ukrainian Nationalist forces.

The Nachtigall Battalion

Formation of the first Ukrainian Battalion, given the code-name Nachtigall, began in April 1941, in Krakow, Poland. The recruitment of volunteers and formation of the Battalion was conducted by the military leadership of the OUN-B, headed by Lt. Roman Shukhevych. Local OUN-B "cells" in eastern Galicia were ordered to select volunteers among their members and send them to Krakow, where they would be vetted by a commission selected by the OUN-B. Those who successfully completed the vetting process and passed their medical examination were sent to Neuhammer, Silesia for basic military training to be conducted by officers of the German Wehrmacht.

In Neuhammer, the new recruits were organized into three companies all placed under the command of Roman Shukhevych. The Battalion's training lasted from the beginning of May 1941 through June 17. After completing the prescribed basic military training program, each member of the Battalion took an oath to participate in the coming military struggle against Soviet Russia, sacrifice his life, if necessary, and secure a free and independent Ukraine. Both Mykola Lebed and Oleksa Havrysh, members of the OUN-B leadership, were present during the oath-taking ceremony in Neuhammer.

The Roland Battalion

The Roland Battalion, also referred to as Group South, was mobilized and began training somewhat later, after the Nachtigall Battalion had already completed its basic training. The Roland Battalion was formed in Austria. Its members were mostly Ukrainian students, who were attending universities in Vienna and other Austrian cities.

The Roland Battalion, a lightly-armed infantry battalion, was commanded by Major Yevhen Pobihushchy, a veteran officer of the Polish Army during the First World War. The Battalion's recruits underwent a six-week basic training program in the village of Saubendorf, south of Vienna. They continued their training during the Battalion's advance through Romania and southwestern Ukraine. The battalion's objective was to meet up with the Nachtigall Battalion in Kyiv in July 1941, and join in declaring support for the Ukrainian government and its authorities.

The Nachtigall Battalion's March on Lviv

On June 18, 1941, the Nachtigall Battalion boarded a transport train in Neuhammer for Rzeszow, a town in eastern Poland. After arriving in Rzeszow, we began marching eastward toward the Soviet border. Our Battalion and the First Battalion of the Brandenburg Corps were attached to the First Mountain Division, commanded by Lt. General Ritter von Lash. We crossed the Buh River at 3:15 a.m. on June 22, 1941, and our two battalions were ordered to advance toward the Soviet sector of the city of Peremyshl. We crossed the San River into Soviet-held territory near the village of Volovyi, not far from Peremyshl. The German-Soviet war had begun! From the village of Volovyi we began our advance toward the city of Lviv.

The First Battalion's assignment was to attack the Soviet defensive line surrounding Lviv from the north. Our Battalion was directed to move forward along the front line as the First Battalion's reserve. We were assigned to clear the road of civilian traffic and any other obstructions, and provide cover for the First Mountain Division, which was coming under heavy air bombardment by the Soviets. Our Battalion's first contact with the Soviet enemy occurred near the village of Zhenena Polska, the location of the Soviet defensive line. There, the First Mountain Division came under fierce artillery fire. This is when we first saw dead and wounded Soviet soldiers and disabled Soviet vehicles and tanks.

The march toward Lviv seemed to us to be advancing much too slowly. Perhaps it was because we were hearing frightening rumors that the NKVD was executing Ukrainians being held in its prisons before abandoning the city. We were becoming more and more frustrated, realizing that we would not get to Lviv in time to prevent any more executions of our people by the NKVD. Had our Battalion been able to reach Lviv sooner, we might have been able to prevent the massacre of at least some of the Ukrainian inmates held in Soviet prisons. Unfortunately, we did not.

Both the Nachtigall and the First Battalion halted their advance in the evening hours of June 29, just a few kilometers east of the Lviv airport. Soviet resistance had weakened considerably during the day, and the last Soviet artillery fire we heard occurred around six o'clock on the following evening, June 30.

Here, I will quote from the report of the **commander of the First Battalion of Brandenburg Corps D.o.D. 800 and of the Nachtigall Battalion**, concerning the night of June 29:

> ... on 29 June 1941, in the evening, I went to General-Adjutant von Lantz's quarters and suggested that we occupy Lviv during the night, as the Soviets had already pulled their forces out of the city. General von Lantz rejected my recommendation, fearing a Soviet ambush. I returned to my group and gave both Battalions the order to stand down. I was convinced that the First Mountain Division would not enter Lviv until late morning at the earliest.
>
> During the night, however, I received further information concerning mass executions taking place in Lviv. Some of this information was furnished by scouts from the Nachtigall Battalion, sent to reconnoiter the Lviv area. I recall speaking with adjutant Dr. Hertzner, who told me that he had

15

also received news of mass executions. The increasing frustration of his soldiers was understandable.

Having received further updates around midnight, June 29 to 30, concerning the situation in Lviv, I decided unilaterally to enter the city that night, to prevent the further massacre of civilians. I ordered both of my Battalions, which I previously ordered to stand down, to prepare for an immediate march on Lviv. I also decided not to inform the divisional command of my unilateral action.

The three companies of our Battalion reached the northwestern city limits after midnight. We were dispatched to various strategically important locations in the city, including the radio station, electric power station, railway station, and citadel. Members of the Nachtigall Battalion were sent to secure the NKVD prisons, where many inmates had been murdered. Together with other members of the Battalion, we occupied the building adjacent to the St. Yurii Cathedral. That was at 3:00 a.m.

The rest of our Battalion entered the city at 4:30 a.m. on June 30. Upon entering the city, our Battalion was divided into several groups. Part of the First Company was sent to St. Yurii Cathedral. A second group, from the First Company, was sent to the prisons on Lontzki and Pelczynska Streets. The Second and Third Companies were sent to the Zamarstyniv District, where they surrounded the prison and secured the natural gas works.

Members of the First Company reached the Cathedral at 5:30 a.m. Soon, the square in front of the Cathedral began to fill with the city's Ukrainian residents. They had arrived to greet "their" army.

At 6:30 a.m., Metropolitan Andrej Sheptytsky received a delegation from our Battalion, headed by Company Commander, Roman Shukhevych. The Metropolitan, who was paralyzed and unable to walk, was carried to the balcony of the Cathedral. From there he spoke to the assembled soldiers and bestowed his Pastoral Blessing on us, in the presence of thousands of the city's faithful. Around 7:00 a.m., two Soviet fighter planes flew over the square and began firing into the crowd. Luckily, there were no casualties.

At about 8 a.m. we received confirmation of the brutal murders of inmates in the prison on Lontzki Street. Some of the Battalion's members went there. One of those to go was Roman Shukhevych. He discovered the body of his younger brother, Yurii, among the many inmates who had been murdered by the NKVD. The scene at the Lontzki Street prison was horrible: the prison cells and corridors were stacked full of dead bodies. One had to climb over them to get from one cell to the next. The bodies had begun to decompose, and the stench was unbearable. The scenes in the other prisons of Lviv were equally gruesome.

Around 10:30 a.m. our unit, which had been stationed at the Cathedral, was ordered to march to the Rynok (Market Square), the site of the City Hall. We ate breakfast in the field kitchen which had been set up in the square. Earlier, members of the First Company had been ordered to go to the prisons on Lontzki and Pelczynska Streets with instructions to keep civilians from entering the prisons. The First Company was finally relieved by German police units at 10:00 a.m. on the following day, July 1. Our Battalion was quartered at the Second German Gymnasium on Valy Street. We were relieved by German units later the same day and received an unexpected, but very welcome furlough for the next few days.

The previous day, June 30, members of the OUN-B proclaimed

17

the re-establishment of an Independent Ukraine at a solemn gathering at the Prosvita (Enlightenment) Society. An interim government was formed, headed by Yaroslav Stetsko. Our Battalion was represented at the meeting by Commander Roman Shukhevych, who was appointed Deputy Minister of Military Affairs in the interim government. July 6, our Battalion left Lviv and headed east toward the city of Ternopil.

Continuing from an excerpt of the **Battalion commander's statement** concerning during his interrogation by the Allies after the War:

> During the next few hours, I continued to receive reports from the Nachtigall and Brandenburg Battalions. They had been sent into the city to gather intelligence. My command post remained at the Cathedral until 8:00 a.m. the following day, until it was moved to the City Hall. There, I increased my staff. I ordered my adjutant, Hertzner, to recall all of the companies of the Nachtigall Battalion from the various posts which they were guarding and to assemble them in the square facing City Hall.
>
> A crowd of several thousand civilians had gathered in the square. Most of them were Ukrainians. When the Nachtigall Battalion entered the square the people greeted them enthusiastically. Some in the crowd even got on their knees and prayed. The soldiers of the Nachtigall Battalion began singing patriotic Ukrainian songs to the joyful tears of the people in the square. The scene touched me to the depths of my soul.
>
> Sometime before noon, Dr. Hartman, Commander of the First Company of the Brandenburg Battalion, came to report that his Company, which was guarding one of the NKVD prisons in the city, had

discovered mounds of dead bodies of prison inmates. When I heard this, I decided to visit the scene for myself and ordered Hartman and Drs. Treubes and Benkelberg to accompany me to the prison.

I don't remember which prison it was, where it was located, or what it looked like. I do remember that there must have been a fire burning in the prison, because I was repelled and driven back by the smell of putrid smoke and the stench of burning, decomposing bodies. I was literally unable to enter the prison.

Commanders Treubes and Benkelberg did enter the prison and later prepared a written report. They detailed their findings concerning the dead bodies in the prison. Still later, I received additional reports concerning mass murders of prisoners in other prisons in the city.

From the reports I received from Professor Oberlander, I learned that some of the victims murdered in the NKVD prisons were relatives of members of the Ukrainian Nachtigall Battalion.

Later that afternoon, the city of Lviv began to take on a very different appearance. The city's streets began filling with our marching troops and cheering residents, who felt safe.

Now that Lviv was no longer in the hands of the Soviets, that day or the next, July 1, I recalled all of the units of the Brandenburg and Nachtigall Battalions from the various strategic points which they had been guarding or occupying in the city. Their duties were assumed by other units.

During the short time that the two Battalions which

I commanded were stationed in Lviv, it was becoming increasingly difficult to understand who was supposed to be giving orders. Commander Hertzner was giving me detailed periodic reports and was the first officer to inform me that civilians, mostly Jews, were being mistreated. This was being done primarily by the civilian German authorities, who had assumed control of Lviv, and by special units of the Sonderkommando.

I specifically asked Commander Hertzner whether anyone from my Battalions had participated in abusive conduct toward civilians, including Jews. He emphatically replied, 'No!' Later that day, on July 5, as my staff and I were leaving Lviv by car for the city of Ternopil, Hertzner reported that the Nachtigall Battalion had yet to fire its first round.

I knew Hertzner to be an honest and reliable individual and had no reason to doubt him. While I was still in Lviv, I sent Captain Tuna, my second deputy, to accompany Adjutants Holman and Kershner on their patrol of the city and evaluation of the existing circumstances.

Every officer reported to me on a daily basis. They indicated with disgust that in some parts of the city there was much chaos, and that the Einsatzgruppen had 'begun their work.'

I sent my report to Admiral Canaris via my personal chauffeur. I emphasized that the existing chaos in Lviv and the acts of brutality were being committed by the Einsatzgruppen against civilians, assisted in some instances by soldiers of the regular army.

I must acknowledge that some units of the German

Army were not properly disciplined. The Slovak unit, which entered Ternopil, behaved like a gang of thieves and robbers. Some Austrian troops from the Fourth Mountain Division in Ternopil area behaved with particular brutality toward the civilian population, especially toward the Jews. In Ternopil, I heard that soldiers of the SS Viking Division had murdered hundreds of Jews.

I never gave any order or directive to Commander Hertzner or to any of the officers of the Nachtigall Battalion to abuse, brutalize, or otherwise mistreat civilians. Nor did I permit them to seize, appropriate, or steal the property of civilians.

I never received a single report suggesting that anyone in the Nachtigall Battalion had committed any such shameful act. Of course, I cannot testify that a member of the unit, acting entirely on his own, could not have committed an unauthorized criminal act against civilians.

It must be clear to everyone that during the occupation of a large city such as Lviv, where large numbers of troops, along with the Gestapo and members of the Party, were arriving and assembling, the situation was truly chaotic. This severely limited the ability of the responsible authorities to maintain civil order and prevent criminal activity.

I believe that the Commander of the Nachtigall Battalion gave an accurate and truthful account of the activities of the Battalion during its brief stay in Lviv.

We were quickly relieved by German units and recalled to the City Square after successfully occupying and securing various strategic points in the city. The rest of our time in Lviv we spent on leave. Prior to taking advantage of our furlough we were given a strict order by Commander Roman Shukhevych: to follow no orders or directives from any German officer, but to await further orders from our Ukrainian commanders!

Freed from our duties for the remainder of the week, we wanted to visit our families and friends. One soldier from the First Company addressed Commander Shukhevych with a request that he be allowed to visit his family in the countryside, not far from the city. Commander Shukhevych rebuked him sharply, "What's the matter with you? Do you also want to disappear into the countryside like they did in 1918?" Shukhevych was referring to the tens of thousands of soldiers from the Army of the Ukrainian National Republic who failed to return to their units after going home on furlough. The desertions of so many soldiers had fatal consequences for the Ukrainian Army's ability to oppose the superior forces of Trotsky's Red Army. The better-disciplined, better-fed and better-armed Red Army soon defeated the greatly reduced Ukrainian forces, bringing an end to Ukraine's short-lived independence.

Hearing Shukhevych's sharp rebuke, nobody else in the Battalion dared ask him for permission to visit family in the countryside. Those of us with relatives or friends in the city were allowed to visit them. Many of us ran into old friends and colleagues from school. Those who were in Lviv for the first time were able to visit the city's many churches, monuments, museums, parks, and other places of interest. Our pleasant furlough came to an end all-too-quickly, however, and we left Lviv for the city of Ternopil on the morning of July 7.

The Nachtigall Battalion in Lviv, July 1941

I'd like to share some recollections of several of my comrades from the Nachtigall Battalion concerning our brief stay in Lviv:

Stepan Kostelanetz recalled the following:

> The road to Lviv was filled with military transport vehicles. We entered the city in the early morning hours of June 30. Several buildings in the city were still burning. Groups of frightened people were slowly crawling out from wherever they had hidden during the Soviet evacuation of Lviv. On my second day in the city I went to the Brygidka Prison, where I witnessed a macabre scene. Amid the stench coming from hundreds of decomposing bodies, I heard sobs of women and children, who were looking for their loved ones among the dead. Many of the victims had their skulls crushed, eyes gouged out, noses cut off, or arms and legs broken.

> Some prison cells had been cemented shut by the Soviets and were literally packed full of corpses. The frightening scene was far worse than anything out of Dante's *Inferno*. I was present when Commander Roman Shukhevych discovered the body of his younger brother, Yurii. The terrible images from the Brygidka Prison during those first days of July 1941, will remain in my memory until the day I die.

> It was my first time in Lviv. Along with my comrades, I went sightseeing in the "City of Lions," so dear to all of us. We went to the St. Yurii Ukrainian Greek Catholic Cathedral, Sokil Square, Vysoky Zamok (High Castle), Stryjsky Park, and

the Wallachian Church. There was so much to see and admire. For a brief time we were able to forget about the terrible events of the past few days.

At the Wallachian Church, I spoke with Father Zyatyk, a professor at the Theological Academy. He tearfully described how the Soviets had herded the Academy's faculty members and students together and threatened to shoot them all, and how all of the teachers and students prayed fervently in silence.

Many of the residents of Lviv, who had lived for the previous two years under harsh Soviet occupation, were overjoyed to see us, their "own" army, marching through the city. News of our arrival spread quickly, and groups of young men and women soon began streaming into Lviv from neighboring towns and villages. Many arrived on bicycles to see their friends, brothers, or sweethearts. Others just came to see the new "Ukrainian army." I ran into a number of my old friends from the towns of Komarno, Bartkiv, Boryslav and Drohobych. Uppermost on the minds of a great many young men was the simple question: "When can I join the Ukrainian Army?" Those were moments of great joy, but they were tempered by grief. The heartfelt greetings, warm embraces, and tears of joy of the city's residents were tempered by the sorrowful knowledge that so many Ukrainians had been murdered in the city's prisons and jails by the fleeing Soviet NKVD.

Several of my friends and I had a very unpleasant experience on our first day in Lviv. Some residents started looting the city's shops, grabbing anything they could get their hands on. As several of my comrades and I entered a sporting goods store in process of being looted, we saw the fierce determination of the looters to take something. So, we simply decided to hand over goods to the looters, to stop them from wrecking the whole store. Somehow, we had not seen the notice posted at the entrance to the store, declaring that the door had been officially sealed. Soon we were surrounded by the German Military Police and placed under arrest while the looters fled, leaving us to face the consequences.

We were eventually released, but our identification documents were confiscated. Naturally, we were afraid that we would be court-martialed for "theft of Government Property." But fate was kind to us this time. The officer who had taken our documents and his driver were killed when their vehicle ran over a land mine, and all of our documents were destroyed in the ensuing explosion. We received new identification documents, just before our company was loaded onto transport trucks and began heading further east.

K. Talanchuk made the following entry in his diary concerning his experiences at the time:

The war began in the pre-dawn hours of 22 June, 1941. The first line of the Wehrmacht advanced forward quickly, stopping briefly in the Yaniv Forest.

Our Battalion was driven by truck to the village of Krakivtsi, from where we began our march toward Lviv. Shortly before 4:00 a.m., we reached Lviv and stopped for a short break at the tollgate on Yaniv Street.

During the break Commander Shukhevych asked who among us knew the city well, as we had to get to the St. Yurii Cathedral by the quickest and safest route in order to protect the Cathedral from a possible Soviet attack. I was somewhat surprised that no one came forward, as I thought that several of the men were from Lviv. So I decided to step forward and said that I knew the city well. Shukhevych asked me which route I would recommend and when I answered to his apparent satisfaction, he ordered me to "take the Battalion and lead."

The Battalion followed me in full combat readiness. We safely reached the square facing the Cathedral without encountering the enemy and assembled at the front gate of the Cathedral. People were beginning to gather in the square in large numbers. They greeted us enthusiastically, giving us bouquets of flowers, embracing us, and showering us with kisses. They were overjoyed to see "their" Ukrainian Army. We were told by many people that the Soviets had been gone for three days, leaving hundreds of murdered victims in the prisons.

Our Battalion marched through the Cathedral gate and into the courtyard to await Metropolitan Andrej Sheptytsky's appearance. The Metropolitan soon appeared on the balcony and greeted us warmly. He spoke to us about our solemn duty to defend our people. Then he administered his Pastoral Blessing upon us. It was a very moving and memorable moment.

Commander Shukhevych then took the second rii (unit) of the First Company of our Battalion to the prison on Lontzki Street. There, we found many murdered inmates. Among the dead was Yurii Shukhevych, our Commander's younger brother. Every one of us sympathized deeply with him. We remained at the prison until noon, when we were relieved by a German unit and taken to a military depot in a newer part of Lviv and ordered to guard it.

There was a garage on the premises where several Soviet ZIS (Zavod imeni Stalina – Stalin Factory) trucks were parked. All of the ZIS trucks ran on generators powered by steam, which was produced by burning wood. Automobile and truck parts were scattered everywhere. I asked the mechanics whether the ZIS motors could be modified to make them run on gasoline. They assured me that it wouldn't be a problem, and in a couple of hours I had a nice three-ton truck which ran on gasoline. I thanked the mechanics for their quick work, and they were happy that they had been able to do me a favor.

That evening, our group no longer had to walk the streets of Lviv. We rode to our assigned quarters in the Temni Valy (Dark Fortifications) section of the city in the ZIS truck. I was entrusted with the ZIS and became our Battalion's "official chauffeur." We decorated our truck with our unofficial emblem on the cabin doors: a singing Nachtigall (nightingale) perched on a tree branch. Incidentally, I want to emphasize that none of the Ukrainian officers, nor the non-commissioned officers in our Battalion wore insignia of any kind. We were dressed in the standard uniform of the Wehrmacht, but without any markings or insignia.

Driving around Lviv in the course of performing my assignments, I had several unforgettable experiences with my ZIS. On level streets it drove quite well. Uphill, however, it resisted like a stubborn mule and would simply refuse to move. I remember one specific incident as I was driving uphill on Stryjska Street. Approaching Kosynerska Street, my "mule" suddenly stopped and refused to budge. So, I backed up about twenty meters and stopped. I gassed the engine and moved forward about twenty meters. The ZIS stalled again. I repeated the procedure ten times, with the same result every time! In the end, I had no choice but to back up all the way to Pelczynska Street. There, I stopped for a while and let the engine cool-off. I restarted the engine, punched the accelerator and finally drove off. I religiously avoided the hilly streets of Lviv from then on!

During the time that I had stopped, several mechanics had approached the truck and began examining the motor but couldn't find anything wrong with it. No one was able to solve the mystery. Why did the ZIS keep stalling?

When the time came for our Battalion to leave Lviv for the East, my skin began to tingle. How would I ever get up the hill on Lychakivska Street to the Vynnyky area? Luckily, I was able to follow a convoy of vehicles going downhill to the same area where I was going. But once I got there, the engine began to sputter again. I kept worrying all the way to the village of Slovity, near the town of Zolochiv, some twenty miles from Lviv.

In Slovity, I drove onto a freshly mowed clover lawn next to the parish church and parked the truck.

Our Platoon immediately went in search of something to eat, while I began tinkering with the ZIS' motor. I took it apart but couldn't find anything wrong with it, so I put it back together. I poured some oil and gasoline into the engine and turned the ignition key. This time it wouldn't even start! Frustrated and exhausted, I walked away and just went to sleep. In the meantime, our convoy had continued on, leaving us behind!

On Sunday morning, Genko Lobay brought me some breakfast. Once I had eaten, it dawned on me to check the truck's fuel line. I unscrewed the fuel line and discovered that it was plugged with cotton wadding! I removed the wadding, cleaned out the line as best I could and screwed the cap back on. That took all of half an hour. But this time, the engine started up right way and we were ready to go! I later heard that many Red Army truck drivers stuffed their vehicle's fuel line to avoid retreating with the rest of their unit.

My deputy, **Anton Fedenyshyn**, recalled his experiences in Lviv as follows:

As we approached the outskirts of Lviv, we were ordered to stop and bivouac for the night. During the night, however, we were suddenly awakened and ordered to resume our march. We entered the city by Horodysky Street. Lt. Pavlyk called me over and ordered me to drive Lt. Oberlander, our German liaison officer, to the center of the city.

Dawn was just breaking, and the streets of Lviv were still empty when Oberlander and I approached the Ratusha (City Hall). My heart fluttered when I saw the blue and yellow Ukrainian flag flying over the building! From City Hall we drove to the prison on Zamartynivka Street, where I ran into an old friend from school. He was standing at the front gate. I asked him to let my brother, who lived in the area, know that I was alive and well and in the city with my unit. While I was there, more and more people were gathering in front of the prison. Lt. Oberlander then asked to be driven to the St. Yurii Cathedral. We drove to the gate in front of the Cathedral and proceeded into the courtyard. There, we found Father Clement Sheptytsky, the Metropolitan's brother, pacing back and forth and reciting the Rosary. We asked him about his and his brother's health and left.

We returned to City Hall, where we met our soldiers from the Second Company. Lt. Oberlander asked me to drive him to the Vokzal (Railroad Station) so that he could ascertain the situation there. We found the Vokzal completely empty; there was absolutely nobody around.

From the Vokzal, Oberlander decided to return to City Hall. I asked to be dropped off on Piariv Street, close to where my brother lived. Oberlander agreed and dropped me off near some garages, which appeared to be automotive repair shops. By that time, it was already getting lighter outside, and large numbers of people were beginning to come out into the streets. When they saw us, their own "Nightingales," they waved and shouted words of welcome!

After visiting with my brother briefly, I returned to the garages which I had seen earlier and asked about the possibility of getting an automobile. I was told that there was an automobile in the garage which had been assigned to the Soviet Academy of Foreign Trade. I immediately commandeered the car, a pretty little cherry-red Chevrolet, and used it to drive Lt. Oberlander around town. I kept the Chevy during my entire stay in Lviv and used it to go wherever I needed. I was still driving the car around town after my unit had left Lviv for Ternopil!

Members of the Organization of Ukrainian Nationalists proclaimed an Independent Ukrainian State on June 30, 1941. Our Battalion marched before the Prosvita Building on Market Square, where the Proclamation was read to the citizens gathered in the Square. It was packed with people, proudly singing patriotic songs. It was an extraordinarily emotional moment! Some people were kneeling on the pavement, tears streaming down their faces, thanking the Almighty for liberating them from Soviet occupation. The Ukrainian residents of Lviv looked upon our Battalion as their savior. Little did they realize then that the Nazis would soon begin imposing their own brand of brutal tyranny!

Sunday, my Company attended the Divine Liturgy at the Church of the Transfiguration. We marched to the church along Ruska Street, singing all the way. As we marched, the people of the city waved to us, cheering, as they had from the moment they first saw our Battalion earlier that morning. Later in the afternoon most of the members of our Battalion attended the funeral of Yurii Shukhevych, our Commander's younger brother. Yurii had been one of those imprisoned and murdered by the NKVD before it fled the city. A large number of people attended his funeral. Yurii Shukhevych was laid to rest in the famous Lychakiv Cemetery. Details of the funeral have faded from my memory, but I remember that our Commander continued to wear a black mourning band on the left sleeve of his uniform for a long time after his brother's death.

When German units relieved us of guard duty at the various strategically important locations throughout the city, we were given an unexpected but welcome furlough for the next several days. Many of us used the opportunity to visit loved ones, old friends and acquaintances, or to make new friends. We were determined to make the most of our brief stay in Lviv. Before we went into the city, however, Roman Shukhevych, our commander, warned us not to follow any orders from German officers, and not to seek revenge against anyone. During the remainder of our stay in Lviv, we were invited to many homes and were graciously received by our hosts.

Part of our Battalion was quartered at the 4th German Gymnasium, together with some German units. The Germans had placed their weapons against some kozly (sawhorses) standing in front of the Gymnasium. Some of our boys decided to take advantage of the situation and quietly "exchanged" their own inferior weapons for the better ones stacked by the Germans in front of the building. One of our men even "found" an MP, a highly-valued automatic pistol, which belonged to some hapless German soldier. The rest of our Battalion was housed in a hotel at the corner of Copernicus and Syxtuska Streets. During the third or fourth day of our furlough we received blue and yellow colored bands (the Ukrainian national colors) and were told to sew them on the epaulettes of our uniforms.

I drove through the city of Lviv several times a day, but I did not see any dead bodies on the streets of the city, or hanging from balconies, as some witnesses produced by the Soviets have claimed. This was part of an ongoing and well-orchestrated effort to defame Ukrainian opponents of the Soviet regime. The Soviets wanted to cover up or at least divert attention from their own crimes and atrocities, committed as they fled from Lviv during the last days of June 1941. Every soldier in the Nachtigall Battalion had been given a direct, specific and emphatic order by Commander Roman Shukhevych: "Do not cover your hands with the blood of others... Do not commit any crimes or carry out any acts of reprisal or vengeance!" His order was clear and unequivocal and absolutely binding on every member of the Battalion!

East of the River Zbruch

Our Battalion arrived in Ternopil sometime around three o'clock on July 5. We were greeted with flowers by several representatives of the city's administration. The city had a very sad, desolate appearance. The windows in many of its buildings had been blown out by Soviet bombs. Two days earlier, the German Sonderkommando had shot many of Ternopil's Jewish residents.

On July 6, we were awakened about five o'clock in the morning and instructed to prepare to leave Ternopil without delay. We would be going on to the town of Hrymailiv. Two of our Battalion's Companies were ordered to continue going east, while the third Company was left behind, in reserve. Our Companies were joined by a German company consisting of several units equipped with superior artillery.

We resumed our march eastward as an advance security force, and Commander Heinz assumed command of our Battalion. East of Hrymailiv we crossed the Zbruch River and continued in the same direction, passing through the towns of Sataniv, Yarmolyntsi, Derezhnya, Vovkovyntsi, Zhmerynka and Brailiv before reaching the city of Vinnytsia. From Vinnytsia we expected to continue marching on to Kyiv, some 300 kilometers farther. There, we anticipated witnessing the solemn proclamation of Ukraine's Independence, and offering our support to the new interim Ukrainian government.

Not far from the town of Derezhnya we passed the so-called "Stalin line." At dawn on the following day we assembled in battle formation, together with several German units. At 9:00 a.m., shortly after breakfast, we began advancing eastward, intending to penetrate and repel the "Stalin line". Our advance was accompanied by a thunderous artillery barrage launched by the German Army, firing from some distance behind us. The artillery barrage included cannon fire from 42 cm. "Big Berthas" and was augmented by heavy bombardments from German aircraft. By noon the road east was open again. The Soviet defenders, who had been firing from bunkers, surrendered. During our breakthrough the continuous shooting and explosions of bombs produced a horrendous roar. The scene was made even more hellish by the flames of the *Flammenverfere* (flamethrowers).

After we had broken through several rows of bunkers the road ahead lay wide open, and our Battalion was able to resume its advance without further resistance from the enemy. It was only on the road from Proskuriv (today, Khmelnytsky) to Vinnytsia, on the Brailiv plateau, that we again encountered heavy fire from the Soviets. Our forward advance units were met by fierce machine gun fire from the retreating Soviets, and the ferocity of the gun fire suggested a full regiment of defenders. Colonel Kratochville, who commanded our combined Battalions during the advance, sent out a 20-man reconnaissance team led by Lt. Oberlander to survey the alternate road from the town of Bar to Brailiv. Oberlander took

34

Lieutenant Yurii Lopatynsky with him as his interpreter. This is what **Yurii Lopatynsky** wrote about that reconnaissance mission:

> We drove to Brailiv in two vehicles. On the outskirts of town we stopped to make some inquiries. The residents who lived along the road on which we were traveling looked at us with great curiosity. This was probably the first time they had seen 'Germans'.
>
> I approached an elderly man sporting a Cossack mustache and asked him: 'Old man, are the Soviets still in town?' Visibly agitated, he responded: 'Don't go there. There are more than six hundred of them.' Ignoring his warning, however, we got back into our vehicles and continued onward. A few minutes later, after crossing the bridge over the pond and climbing the hill, we were suddenly 'welcomed' by a volley of heavy machine gun fire.

The truck I was riding in veered off the road and into a ditch. We jumped out and hid behind an embankment, from which we returned fire. The Soviet machine gunners were positioned next to a sugar mill, and some of them were loading sacks of sugar into wagons. Our second vehicle remained stranded on the bridge. We maintained our position for several hours and were able to turn back the Soviet attack. But two of our men were killed, and three others were wounded. We retreated to the Proskuriv-Vinnytsia highway and rejoined our column, which was assembling on the road.

> Suddenly, about thirty Soviet fighter planes appeared from nowhere and began strafing our column with heavy machine gun fire and dropping bombs on us. The Soviet planes repeated their attack eight times during the next couple of hours

and killed more than fifty German soldiers. They also destroyed a number of army vehicles. Fortunately for us, no one in our Battalion was killed.

When we were last reading **K. Talanchuk's** account, he was still fixing his ZIS truck when his unit departed for Ternopil, leaving him behind. I'd like to quote some additional passages from his recollections, showing how he got back to his unit:

At noon, our squad resumed its advance eastward, continuously looking for our Battalion. We drove through the town of Zolochiv and on to Ternopil, where we stopped again to inquire about our Battalion. We were told that it had continued on, so we remained in Ternopil until that evening. We had driven only about three kilometers out of town when we got a flat tire. I started removing the tire but couldn't, as the threads on one of the bolts were worn off. I couldn't get the last nut off, and all I had was a jack, a hammer and pliers. Luckily one of our men had a bicycle, so I borrowed it and rode back to Ternopil, where I had seen a blacksmith's shop along the road. I borrowed a chisel from the blacksmith and returned to our vehicle. I broke off the bolt, removed the tire from a vehicle in the ditch and put it on our vehicle. We spent that night in our truck and continued eastward the next morning.

When we came to the intersection Skalat-Pidvolochysk we approached some villagers who were milling around. We asked them whether they had seen our unit, the one with the insignia of a bird (our Nightingale) on its doors. They believed that it had continued on to Skalat but weren't sure. When we got to Skalat we started asking around for our unit, but the residents said they hadn't seen it. We also asked for something to eat and were generously fed by the villagers. Afterwards, we continued on to the town of Pidvolochysk. When we got there, we found no trace of our unit. A battle was raging somewhere near the Zbruch River. We continued driving to within a couple of kilometers of the river and settled in for the night. There were German troops all around us, but still no sign of our group.

Famished, we again began looking for something to eat. I remember walking into a farmhouse of an obviously prosperous homestead. Inside were an old grandfather and grandmother, their daughter or daughter-in-law, and a teenage granddaughter. I asked if we could get something to eat. They readily gave me some supper, and the grandfather instructed his granddaughter, 'Halya, bring a loaf of bread and some salo (bacon).' I wanted to pay them, but the grandfather refused to take any money. Instead, he invited me to stop in again if I happened to be in the area. I thanked him for the delicious meal and for his warm hospitality and invitation to visit again. That night my comrades and I slept on the roof of our truck, under the bright stars. In the morning we continued on to Pidvolochysk. My comrades went ahead to "organize" something for breakfast. They found a box of eggs hidden behind the plaster wall of an abandoned home. We boiled the eggs and ate them. They were simply delicious!

When we came to the road intersection for Vinnytsia, Bar, and Berdychiv, we saw a ZIS truck exactly like mine driving along the road. We looked closer. Standing on a small stool perched on the running board and bent over, apparently looking at the motor, was a non-commissioned officer from our unit, a Czech by nationality. Actually, he was pouring gasoline into the carburetor from a glass bottle. Sitting behind the steering wheel was our own Myrosyo Kalba! When he saw me, Kalba asked me to drive because I was more familiar with its idiosyncrasies. I didn't want the vehicle to stop in the road, however, and took over the functions of the Czech "gasoline attendant" while Myrosyo Kalba continued driving the vehicle.

Along the way, we were met by the Melder (messenger) from our unit, on his motorcycle. He informed us that our unit was just a kilometer away, in the nearby woods. Rather than rejoining our unit right then, we drove to the village and parked our truck. The guys went to get something to eat, while I started working on the truck. We didn't realize that Soviet troops were still hunkered down at the other end of the village and in the adjacent fields. We spent the night in the village and rejoined our unit the next morning. Commander Shukhevych and our "boys" were all there, waiting for us.

Our commanders ordered the Second Company from Brandenburg Corps D.o.D. 800 into action against the enemy. One platoon of the Second Company, commanded by Lieutenant Luther, was ordered to "roll up" the enemy's left flank. One of our platoons was sent to "roll up" the enemy's right flank. While advancing toward the Soviet positions, both platoons came under particularly heavy fire. They had unwittingly walked right into the enemy's "horseshoe" and found themselves surrounded by three regiments of Soviet troops! Most of the Soviet troops, it later turned out, were young Asian recruits.

Luther's platoon attacked and all but one of its members were killed! Fortunately, no one in our unit was killed. On hearing the enemy's loud commands to, "Throw down your arms and surrender!", and exclamations of, "Hurrah for Comrade Stalin and the Communist Party!" our boys jumped down from the truck and ran for cover in the nearby ditch. We "answered" the Soviet troops with such a strong barrage of fire that they quickly lost the appetite to attack and retreated to their trenches. Only one of our soldiers was injured. However, our unit soon came under heavy crossfire from the opposite direction. It came from powerful "Maxim" machine guns firing from the other end of Brailiv, near the sugar mill. So, our platoon had to retreat back down the hill and wait for reinforcements.

Some captured Soviet soldiers were brought to our security unit's command post. To our great surprise none of them spoke or even understood Russian. They were troops from Central Asia. Our chaplain, Rev. Dr. Ivan Hrynyokh, addressed them with the words, 'Salam aleikum" (Peace be with you). Upon hearing this greeting, the prisoners immediately "came to life" and began speaking animatedly. Unfortunately, we couldn't understand them. Eventually, using various hand gestures, diagrams and symbols drawn in the soil, the Soviet POW's were able to show us where the Soviet defensive line was deployed and gave us a good idea of their numerical strength. Only then did we realize that an entire division was facing us! So we dug in, and the shooting began anew. Our orders were to hold our position until dawn, when we would be reinforced. Close to 5:00 a.m. the following morning, the First Mountain Division appeared. After a brief preliminary barrage of artillery fire, we resumed our advance on the Soviet positions.

We followed in the retreating footsteps of the Soviet troops. By 9:00 a.m., we entered Vinnytsia. While approaching the city, we had encountered our first Molotov cocktails. The ditches along the road were full of glass bottles filled with gasoline. The Soviets apparently had planned to use them in defending the city but changed their plans at the last minute and retreated beyond the Buh River. They may have concluded that it would be easier to defend the eastern part of the city from the eastern shore of the river and slow down our advance more effectively from there. During the remainder of the day we were able to occupy only the part of Vinnytsia which lay on the western shore of the Buh River. We could not ford the river because it was coming under continuous and heavy artillery fire, and we had no saper (bridge-building) units with us. When we finally did enter the center of Vinnytsia, we found it deserted. Its shops had been looted, and many of them had been completely destroyed. The Soviets were continuing to bombard the city with heavy artillery fire.

Our Battalion split into smaller groups and began searching the city's buildings. We checked the city headquarters of the NKVD prison cells and the odinochki (solitary cells), which were so small that they could accommodate only one standing prisoner. In the basement of the City Theatre we found a group of actors. They were very surprised to hear us speaking in Ukrainian. We advised all of them to return to their homes and warned the director, who was Jewish, to hide and avoid walking in the streets.

Several days later, our Battalion and the German unit to which we were attached left for the town of Yuzvyn. There, we were given another two-week "rest and relaxation" period. We spent those two weeks driving around the surrounding villages helping the local population organize local councils, since they were now free of the Soviets. We urged the villagers to hide their grain and food supplies from the Germans, who might otherwise requisition them.

Initially, the villagers were distrustful of us. Gradually, however, they realized that we really were Ukrainians and became quite friendly. They started visiting our camp often, bringing us honey, fruits and other treats. The first Sunday during our stay in Yuzvyn, Rev. Dr. Hrynyokh, our chaplain, celebrated the Divine Liturgy at a makeshift field altar which we had built in the village square. Our Battalion choir sang the Liturgy. Hearing that a Liturgy would be celebrated in the village, the residents brought prayer books and various religious items used in the service to the makeshift altar. People had hidden these sacred items when the Soviets came to the village and vandalized the local church. The villagers filled the square the service, joining us in singing the Liturgy. Many of them were visibly moved and wept. From that time on, the villagers' attitude toward us changed completely, and they became very friendly to us.

While in Yuzvyn, we received the disturbing news that eastern Galicia had been annexed to the General Government ruled by Hans Frank, and central and eastern Ukraine had been made a part of the Reichskommisariat, ruled by Erich Koch. Even more disturbing was the news that Stepan Bandera, the leader of the Organization of Ukrainian Nationalists (OUN-B), had been arrested by the Gestapo, along with most of the members of the Ukrainian Provisional Government, including Premier Yaroslav Stetsko. Immediately upon learning of the arrests of our political leadership, Commander Roman Shukhevych sent a sharply worded protest to the High Command of the German Army, declaring that the Nachtigall Battalion was terminating all cooperation with the Wehrmacht.

The days following Shukhevych's protest and declaration were no longer days of "rest and relaxation." Instead, they became days filled with apprehension. Would the German military or political authorities punish us, and if so, what would the punishment be? No one knew what would happen with our Battalion. The stress, nervous tension and dreadful anticipation affected both officers and regular soldiers alike. Every one of us was aware of the possible consequences of our decision: execution at the hands of a German firing squad! The best-case scenario, we thought, would be incarceration in a military prison or concentration camp. We fully understood, however, that our Battalion's short-lived role as German "allies" was finished, and we were prepared for the worst. In August 1941, while the higher German authorities were still considering their response to our Commander's protest and defiant declaration, our Battalion was officially deactivated and removed from the Eastern front. We were sent back to Neuhammer for "additional training", pending the German authorities' decision as to our fate. The regular soldiers of our Battalion were completely disarmed, but our officers were permitted to keep their side-arms. In Neuhammer, relations with the German military command were becoming increasingly tense. During our evening conversations with our officers, we angrily complained about the stupid arrogance of the Germans and the idiotic foolishness of Hitler's policies in Eastern Europe. We all predicted that those policies, and the indecent and brutal behavior of the Germans toward the people whose lands they occupied, would inevitably lead to Germany's defeat.

We immediately resumed "normal training", which consisted primarily of military drills and calisthenics. The German Command organized a shooting competition between German and Ukrainian officers and regular soldiers. Close to fifty of us signed up for the competition. First Place in the pistol competition was taken by Commander Roman Shukhevych. Many of our boys also did well, winning first place in several shooting categories. Sundays, we were restricted to an area within six kilometers of our barracks. The atmosphere was becoming more stressful with every passing day. Conflicts with the German non-commissioned officers arose frequently, although relations with the German officers remained "proper" at all times. Nobody knew how it would all end.

Following are the recollections of **Vasyl Sudyk**, one of the Battalion's members, concerning our second training period in Neuhammer:

> We had no idea what would happen to us or what plans our superiors had. We sat around without any purpose for many weeks. Ever more frequently, we would engage in various "subversive"conversations, not even thinking about the adverse effect it might have on our comrades and the "cause."

> A very good friend of mine, Vasyl Korolyshyn, and I began formulating a plan of action. The plan was to obtain a key to the ammunition depot, take a

large supply of ammunition during the night and leave for Ukraine, to somehow continue the fight for Ukraine's freedom. There were sixteen of us from the Berezhany region and twelve from the Pidhayechyna region who were ready to take part in the plan. I obtained a key to the ammunition depot from a comrade who worked there, and everything was set to go. But nothing came of our plan, which was "sabotaged" by some apples! Here's what happened:

Food at the camp was in extremely short supply, and every one of us was constantly hungry. One evening, several of us sneaked into a farmer's orchard and picked one of his apple trees clean! Each of us ate a bunch of apples right on the spot and loaded the rest into a large bag, which we took back to our barracks. There, we were faced with a practical dilemma: where to hide the apples? We assumed, correctly, that the farmer would file a complaint with our Command, and that the premises would be searched. If the apples were found we would be in a great deal of trouble. Military courts during wartime don't joke about such matters. But it was such a shame to get rid of all those delicious apples! Korolyshyn got the brilliant idea to hide the apples in our Company Commander's room, believing that an officer's quarters would probably not be searched. So, Korolyshyn hid the apples in Commander Vasyl Sydor's room, as he knew him well and often went to his room.

When the farmer filed his complaint with the Commandant, a thorough search of our barrack was made, but of course no apples were found.
Commander Sydor, however, had a suspicion that the "apple caper" must have been our doing and began asking Korolyshyn, "as a friend," to tell

him what was going on. He promised to keep Korolyshyn's answer confidential. Korolyshyn admitted everything, even telling Sydor about our plan to steal the ammunition, arm ourselves, and return to Ukraine. He showed him where he had hidden the apples in Sydor's room. The incident provided everyone with a lot of laughs!

Soon, however, our Battalion Commander, Roman Shukhevych also heard of our plan to requisition ammunition and leave for Ukraine, and about our theft of apples from the orchard. He summoned us to meet with him. We promptly admitted everything. To our great surprise, he did not berate us for our actions but actually commended us for our initiative and willingness to continue the struggle for Ukraine's freedom! He did not, however, let us get away without a stern lecture. He reminded us that our superiors were responsible for all of us, and that when the appropriate occasion arose, they would be the ones to tell us what to do. He made us realize that unauthorized acts or plans, such as ours, might cause irreparable harm to our unit and to our cause. His lecture made us understand that our leadership was responsible for us, and that we must follow their orders.

Meanwhile, in Lviv, the situation was getting worse by the day. The Nazis were carrying out massive arrests and conducting interrogations of thousands of Ukrainian activists and OUN members. During the early part of September, Yurii Lopatynsky and Dr. Hertzner were sent to Berlin. Lopatynsky's assignment was to find out what had happened to our OUN leadership, which had been staying in Berlin. After spending the night at his brother's home, Lopatynsky went the next morning to Stepan Bandera's apartment. There, he found Yaroslav Stetsko, Osyp

Tyushka, Omelyan Antonovych and Bandera's wife. Lopatynsky learned that Bandera and Volodymyr Stakhiv had just gone to speak with Obengruppenfuhrer Mueller, who had requested a meeting with them. Neither Bandera nor Stakhiv returned from the meeting. At about eleven o'clock that evening, the Gestapo came to Bandera's apartment and began searching it. The Gestapo ordered all of the men to accompany them. Lopatynsky, however, convinced the Gestapo that he had come to Berlin 'on official business' with his commander and thus was able to escape arrest.

After returning to Neuhammer from Berlin, Dr. Oberlander, our liaison officer, informed us that we would not be punished. However, he also told us that we would not be discharged from military service and permitted to go home. Rather, our Battalion would be reorganized, renamed, and sent to fight the Soviet partisans! Each one of us would be required to "volunteer" for a one-year tour of duty. Oberlander made it very clear that we had no choice in the matter.

Soon afterwards, we were interviewed by a German military commission from Berlin. Finally, on October 19, 1941, more than two months after the Battalion had been disbanded, we were informed that we would be going to Frankfurt an der Oder that same day. In Frankfurt, we would be joined by members of the disbanded Roland Battalion. Our two battalions would be combined into a single unit and would undergo further training.

Reorganization of the Nachtigall and Roland Battalions into Schutzmannshaftsbattalion-201

Our "decommissioned" Battalion arrived in Frankfurt an der Oder on October 19, 1941. The Roland Battalion arrived two days later. At last, our two Battalions would be combined into one unit, which had been our dream originally. The official name of our new Battalion was Schutzmannshaftsbattalion n. 201. Each member of the Battalion "voluntarily" signed a personal service contract obligating himself to serve one year. No new oath was required.

A new liaison officer, Police Captain Moch, was assigned to the new Battalion. He was assisted by supervisory police personnel. Our Battalion was clothed in green police uniforms, without insignia. Prior to the arrival of the members of the old Nachtigall and Roland Battalions in Frankfurt an der Oder and the organization of Schutzmannshaftsbattalion-201, our leaders had submitted a Memorandum to the High Command of the German Army. It was signed by every member of the new Battalion. The Memorandum specified the terms and conditions under which we would participate in further military action with the German Army. The Memorandum was actually a restatement of Commander Roman Shukhevych's written protest, which he had submitted to the German military authorities the previous August.

The essential provisions of the Memorandum were:

1. The Proclamation of Ukrainian Independence of June 30, 1941, must be recognized by the German government.

2. The leadership of the Organization of Ukrainian Nationalists, led by Stepan Bandera, and members of the Provisional Government, led by Yaroslav Stetsko, must be released from custody.

3. Financial and other aid must be provided to families of all Battalion members, and any arrested family members must be released.

4. Any reorganized Battalion will be restricted to military action only on Ukrainian ethnic territory.

5. The political command of the new Battalion must be Ukrainian.

6. The duties and privileges of Ukrainian command staff members must be equal to those of their German counterparts.

7. Members of the Battalion, having previously sworn their loyalty to Ukraine, were bound by that oath and would not swear loyalty to Germany.

8. The new Battalion would serve on a "contract basis" for a period of one year, with each member of the Battalion signing a contract in his individual capacity.

An officer from the Magdeburg branch of the Security Police arrived in camp on November 1. Our Battalion was ordered to assemble in formation to hear his presentation. After a perfunctory greeting, the officer got "down to business." He claimed to speak on behalf of the pertinent authorities in Berlin and came to give us their response to our Memorandum.

He began slowly reading the various points of our Memorandum and giving us the official response to each. He stated that the leaders of the OUN-B had been arrested for criminal acts, not for political reasons. He said that an investigation of the criminal charges was being conducted, and that we would be informed of the results when it was completed. He informed us that once we completed our retraining, we would be deployed on the Eastern Front. The German authorities, he continued, would not require an oath of loyalty to the Third Reich or the Fuehrer. The officer assured us that our demands concerning economic assistance to our families would be satisfied. With respect to our demand that Ukrainian independence be officially recognized by the German Government, the officer stated that a decision had not yet been made.

Much discussion ensued among the members of our Battalion following the officer's statement. Berlin's response, of course, satisfied none of us. Everyone knew that the arrests of the OUN-B leadership had been for obvious political reasons. All of us expected our treatment at the hands of the Germans to get worse. Nor did we believe that the Germans would honor their most recent assurances about assisting our families. They had amply demonstrated their insincerity earlier, during the period of our cooperation with them.

Deployment of Schutzmannshaftsbattalion-201 to Belarus

Our training in Frankfurt an der Oder continued during the entire winter of 1941-42. Our newly retrained Battalion, the Schutzmannshaftsbattalion-201, left for the Eastern Front on March 19, 1942. We did not return to Ukraine, however, but were deployed to Belarus instead. This was a great disappointment to us, as we had always wanted to serve in our homeland. In Belarus we relieved a Latvian unit that was being transferred to Ukraine.

Schutzmannshafts units were security formations organized to guard and protect roads and bridges in areas of German military action. They enabled the efficient movement of forces, equipment and supplies. With their own staff and officers, the Schutzmannshaftsbattalions were not a part of the Wehrmacht organizationally, but operationally they were subordinated to it.

We were now a security unit rather than a military unit. We realized, however, that our mission in Belarus would not be purely defensive in nature, but would necessitate offensive operations as well. Our assignment would be not only to guard and protect the roads and bridges in our assigned area of Belarus, but also to pursue and eliminate Soviet partisans hiding in the forests. They regularly ambushed German convoys on the country's roads, disrupting and impeding the German Army's advance eastward. We would be engaged in such pursuits regularly during the entire period of our deployment in Belarus.

The main German Command Headquarters was located in the city of Borovky, with military barracks and large ammunition depots nearby. In fact, Borovky was the Wehrmacht's major supply depot for much of the Eastern Front. Our Second Company, under Captain Brygider, was posted at the Command Headquarters. Our other companies were deployed at various outposts located some distance from there. The individual outposts would obtain regular shipments of food, supplies and munitions from Borovky. Thus, the soldiers of the Second Company were required to make frequent deliveries to the individual outposts.

Our companies, platoons, and squads were dispersed throughout the areas surrounding Borovky, Lepelya, Komenya, Zhar, Voronezh, and other nearby towns. Each of the ten or so outposts in our area was in a very precarious position. Spread out over an area of many square miles, isolated and located a considerable distance from Lepelya and Borovky, the outposts were constantly subject to a surprise attack by Soviet partisans. Members of our Battalion manned these outposts, which invariably needed to be more heavily fortified with improved berms, stockades, towers, etc. The surrounding forest also had to be cleared. However, even the added fortifications and clearances did not prevent sporadic night attacks by the partisans. Fortunately, none of our outposts was ever taken by the enemy, although we did suffer casualties in defending them.

Our arrogant German commanding officer, Major Mocha, crudely insulted our Battalion at every turn, apparently because we were non-Aryans, *Untermenschen.* He objected to our singing Ukrainian folk and patriotic songs, and constantly complained that we didn't show "proper respect" for the Third Reich and its Fuhrer. More importantly, he frequently issued orders which made no strategic or tactical sense, simply to prove that he was in charge. One such order, which Mocha issued on October 2, 1942, against the advice of the Ukrainian officers under his command, resulted in the needless death of 22 of our comrades and nine German soldiers. They were ambushed by a group of Soviet partisans while marching toward the base where Mocha's superior officers were stationed. We found their mutilated, naked bodies soon thereafter and buried them in a common soldiers' grave in Borovky. The Soviets hadn't had the decency to simply leave the dead bodies but stripped them naked, taking not only their uniforms but their underwear as well. For added measure, the Soviet partisans sadistically mutilated the bodies! Mocha had insisted on the march for the sole purpose of reporting that our unit, under his command, had earlier that day encountered and defeated a large group of enemy partisans. His vanity and stubbornness caused the lives of thirty-one good soldiers! October 2, 1942, was the single deadliest day for our Battalion. It must be said, however, that the officers of the Wehrmacht stationed in Belarus invariably treated the officers and men of our Battalion with courtesy and respect.

Our eight-month deployment in Belarus provided us with an opportunity to learn the methods and techniques of partisan guerilla warfare, which we would later employ in the Ukrainian Insurgent Army. The Soviet partisans showed us how to use camouflage effectively, how to move quietly through the woods, how to improvise, and how to surprise the enemy. While we had not been pleased with our deployment to Belarus, as it was not home, the experience proved to be invaluable. Frankly, our Battalion's numerous engagements with the Soviet partisans in Belarus proved to be far more meaningful and useful than our aborted campaign in western Ukraine. During our deployment in Belarus we not only effectively performed our duties but gained a wealth of tactical knowledge which was later put to good use in fighting both the Nazis and the Soviets in Ukraine. Not a single military objective which our Battalion had been ordered to protect and safeguard in Belarus was ever seized, destroyed or taken by the enemy!

One last thing that bears mentioning about our Battalion's deployment in Belarus is the close, friendly relationship which we established with the ordinary people of Belarus with whom we dealt. Many of them performed important tasks for us at our outposts and soon became our good friends. They brought us fresh food, helped prepare our meals, did our laundry and often supplied us with valuable intelligence. Although they had been wary of us at first, once they realized that we were Ukrainians fighting for our freedom, their attitude changed completely. While we were certainly glad to be returning to our own homes when our "voluntary" term of duty in the battalion ended, it was difficult to part with our good friends in Belarus! Above all, we were afraid that the Soviets would punish them for "collaborating with the enemy. Late in November 1942, toward the end of our service obligations in Schutzmanshaftbattalion-201, our entire Battalion was taken to Mogilev. There, we were assembled and urged to renew our contract and continue our service with the German security forces. Every single member of the Battalion adamantly refused, despite the Germans' repeated exhortations. In the end, the Germans realized that no manner of inducements or promises would help to convince us to remain, and that we were steadfast in our refusal to renew our contracts. The enraged Sturmbanfuhrer angrily dismissed our troops and invited the Battalion's Ukrainian officers into the dining hall, where he screamed at them, "I could have all of you shot..." Major Pobihushchy stood up and spoke forcefully on behalf of our entire Battalion. He declared that since the specific conditions which we had demanded in exchange for our service had not been met by the German authorities, and our families had not received the assistance which had been promised them, we would not serve a moment longer! The Germans continued shouting for some time, but eventually stopped. They declared in anger and obvious frustration that "the matter would be decided in Berlin."

A few days before Christmas, 1942, the same Gestapo representatives returned to our camp and ordered our Battalion to assemble. They informed us that the Sturmbanfuhrer in Berlin had ordered our Battalion dissolved and its members discharged. Our members, he said, would leave for Lviv the following day. We were required to turn in our uniforms, then we would receive our discharge papers and be allowed to return to our homes. Our officers were to be released last. Our release and departure from Belarus brought a definitive end to the cooperation between the Legion of Ukrainian Nationalists and the German military forces during 1941-42.

While we had not been able to reach Kyiv, Ukraine's capital, nor form the core of a reconstituted Ukrainian National Army, as we had hoped, the Legion of Ukrainian Nationalists succeeded admirably in fulfilling a significant part of its intended purpose. The majority of its officers, non-commissioned officers and regular troops became the officers, commanders and instructors in the Ukrainian Insurgent Army (Ukrayinska Povstanska Armiya - UPA). There, they shared with the new UPA recruits their knowledge of military science and tactics and the invaluable experience which they had acquired during basic training and on the front lines in western Ukraine. Perhaps even more importantly, they were able to impart their knowledge and experience in partisan-guerilla warfare, acquired in the forests of Belarus. The former officers and soldiers of the Nachtigall, Roland and Schutzmannschaftsbattalion-201 continued their heroic struggle for Ukrainian independence against both foreign occupiers of Ukraine, the Germans and the Soviets. The Ukrainian Insurgent Army fought stubbornly against the Gestapo and other German units until 1943, and against the Soviet partisans, the Soviet Red Army, the NKVD, and their communist allies, well into the early 1950s.

PART TWO

Allegations Against the Nachtigall Battalion Concerning the Tragic Events of July 1941 in Lviv

In 1959, the Soviets and their communist allies commenced a coordinated propaganda campaign against the Ukrainian Nachtigall Battalion in connection with the so-called "Oberlander Affair." The Soviets had decided to blame members of the Nachtigall Battalion for crimes which had been committed by the Gestapo in Lviv in July 1941, during the brief time that the Nachtigall Battalion was stationed there.

The Soviets accused the Nachtigall Battalion of murdering a group of Polish academicians and many Jewish residents of Lviv. The murders were actually committed by the Nazi Einsatzgruppen at the direction of the Central Bureau of the Gestapo in Berlin. The Soviet accusations were conveniently based on the fact that the Nachtigall Battalion had been attached administratively to a battalion of Brandenburg Corps D.o.D. 800. This unit had been created within the Wehrmacht for "diversionary" assignments, i.e. to perform acts of sabotage in Soviet-occupied territories in order to weaken Soviet resistance during the German army's invasion. It was erroneously classified by the Allies as an SS organization, which resulted in harsher treatment for its members in Allied prisoner of war camps. The Nachtigall Battalion had been attached to Brandenburg Corps D.o.D 800 simply to hide the fact that Ukrainians were being trained by the German army.

It is essential to note, therefore, that the Nuremberg Tribunal determined that Brandenburg Corps D.o.D. 800 was not a criminal organization. Furthermore, its wartime activities were found to be of a purely military nature during the criminal trial of Otto Skorzeni, former SS Commander of the Dachau concentration camp. This did not prevent the Soviets, bent solely on discrediting Ukrainians who had opposed them during the war, from claiming that the Nachtigall Battalion was also a diversionary unit. They even claimed that the Nachtigall Battalion had been parachuted behind Soviet defensive lines in order to commit acts of sabotage and create havoc. This is simply not true. The Nachtigall Battalion was not trained for diversionary activities and never engaged in such. Its members did not devote a single hour during their training to the study or practical use of diversionary activities, and they were never parachuted anywhere. Of course, the Nachtigall Battalion did participate in the Wehrmacht's invasion of Soviet-occupied Ukraine, advancing eastward with the German army between June 22 and July 15, 1941.

The primary purpose for the Soviet propaganda campaign against the Nachtigall Battalion was to denigrate the Ukrainian independence movement and paint all of its participants as "Nazi Collaborators" and "Enemies of the People." Both of these characterizations were epithets the Communists invariably used to describe anyone who opposed the Soviets.

The Murders of Polish Academics in Lviv

During the Yalta Conference in 1945, shortly before the capitulation of Nazi Germany, the Allies agreed to put the leaders of the Third Reich on trial for war crimes which the Nazis had committed. Not long after Germany's unconditional surrender, the International Military Tribunal in Nuremberg began its investigation of Nazi war crimes and continued its proceedings for a period of eighteen months.

The Soviet Union prepared "scrupulously" for the proceedings of the Nuremberg Tribunal, intending to take advantage of the Tribunal to hide its own atrocities. These included the murders of several thousand Polish army officers in the Katyn Forest and the murders of many thousands of civilians during the Soviet retreat from Lviv and other western Ukrainian cities in the summer of 1941. Prior to fleeing from Lviv and retreating eastward, the Soviets left a bloody trail of thousands of murdered civilians, mostly Ukrainians. Today, it is undisputed that the mutilated bodies of thousands of inmates were found in NKVD prisons in eastern Galicia, Volhynia and other areas which had been under Soviet rule after the Molotov-Ribbentrop Pact of August 1939. These murders occurred prior to the German invasion of the Soviet Union on June 22, 1941. In Lviv alone, there were several thousand victims who had been slaughtered by the Soviet NKVD.

While the Second World War was drawing to a close, the Soviet Union created a so-called "Extraordinary State Commission for the Investigation of Crimes committed by the National Socialists in Lviv and its environs." In its December 23, 1944 issue, the official Soviet government newspaper *Izvestiya* published excerpts of the Commission's report concerning the first days of the German occupation of Lviv in 1941. The report was reprinted in the December 30 issue of *Soviet War News* (No. 1047), a publication distributed by the Soviet Embassy in London, England. The same report was later submitted to the International Military Tribunal in

Nuremberg as evidence of German war crimes.

In its report, the Soviet Extraordinary State Commission concluded that "...all of the killings were committed pursuant to previously developed plans; were ordered by the German Hitlerite government; and were perpetrated by a special organization formed to carry out the killings." The report of the Extraordinary Soviet State Commission listed the names of over one hundred defendants. Not a single name was that of a Ukrainian. Nor was there any mention of the Nachtigall Battalion in the Commission's report.

The Nuremberg Tribunal thoroughly examined the case involving the murders of the Polish academicians in Lviv in July 1941. Several volumes of documents of the Nuremberg proceedings were even published in the Soviet Union. A detailed report concerning the murders appears in the third volume of the publication. The report contained the following statement: "Prior to the occupation of Lviv by the German Gestapo, the German government had prepared lists of Polish academicians to be liquidated. Massive arrests and executions began immediately upon the occupation of the city. The Gestapo arrested..."

This statement is important because it shows that during the proceedings of the Nuremberg Tribunal no one claimed that the Ukrainian Nachtigall Battalion was responsible for any criminal action in Lviv. The statement quoted from the Soviet report restates the findings of the Nuremberg Tribunal: that it was the German Gestapo that murdered the Polish professors, and the Nazis who bore the sole responsibility for the murders. In fact, the Soviet prosecutor at Nuremberg stated the same thing in his summation: "The group of professors was arrested on the basis of lists which had previously been prepared on the instructions of the German government." He specifically named the murderers: the secret German police, the Gestapo.

On February 15, 1946, Smirnov, one of the Soviet representatives at the Nuremberg proceedings, quoted from the report of the Extraordinary State Commission, which concluded that, "...before they even entered Lviv, the Gestapo had compiled lists of prominent academics who were to be killed. Massive arrests and shootings began from the moment the Germans entered the city. The Gestapo arrested professor Tadeusz Boj-Zelenski, a member of the Association of Soviet Writers and author of many literary works; professor Roman Repski of the Medical Institute; professor Wlodimierz Seradski...," etc. Smirnov continued, "Professor Grojer of the Medical Institute in Lviv, who was fortunate enough to escape death, testified before the Commission as follows":

I was arrested at midnight on July 3, 1941, and thrown into the back of a motor vehicle. In it were professors Grek, Boj-Zelenski, and others. We were taken to Abramowicz, the Theological Institute. As we were being led down the hall, members of the Gestapo struck us on the back of our heads with their rifle butts and pulled us by the hair. A little later, I saw the Germans take five professors from Abramowicz. Four of them were carrying the bloodied body of Doctor Ruff's son. Ruff was a well-known surgeon in Lviv, who died during his interrogation. The younger Ruff was a respected physician in his own right. All of the academics/professors were taken, under guard, in the direction of the Kadetska Hill. Fifteen to twenty minutes later, I heard gunshots from the direction where the professors had been led.

We see from the materials cited concerning the killings of the Polish professors in Lviv that the Nuremberg Tribunal determined unequivocally that the lists of names had been prepared on orders of the German Government, and that the executions were carried out by the Gestapo. It is also worth noting here that the report of the Soviet Extraordinary Commission attributed the 1940 massacre of several thousand Polish army officers in the Katyn Forest near

Smolensk, Russia, to the Germans. Only recently has the post-Soviet Russian Government finally acknowledged Soviet responsibility for the Katyn Forest murders. It was a very belated acknowledgment by the Kremlin, coming almost seven decades after the Katyn massacre, and after countless attempts to lay blame for the murders on the Germans.

Attempting to blame the Germans for the Katyn massacre, the Soviet Extraordinary Commission in 1945 boldly alleged, "In order to hide their crimes in the Lviv region, the Hitlerite murderers used the same methods they had used earlier, after they had murdered the Polish officers in the Katyn Forest. The Commission's experts confirmed that the graves in the Lysenytsky Forest near Lviv were camouflaged in exactly the same way as the graves of the Polish officers who had been murdered by the Germans in Katyn." This cynical attempt by the Soviets to hide their murderous actions in Lviv was pointedly rejected by the Nuremberg Tribunal. Particularly significant for our purposes here is the fact that the report of the Soviet Extraordinary Commission concerning the Gestapo's crimes in Lviv made no mention of the Nachtigall Battalion.

There are two other very important documents, both of which are authoritative and credible, that must be considered with respect to the murders of the Polish academics. Both documents originated shortly before or just after the German retreat from Lviv and relied on the testimony of local witnesses. They are: (a) the report of an investigation conducted by Zygmunt Albert, Professor of the Medical Institute in Lviv, who gathered evidence and published it in the periodical *Pzeglond Liekarski* (*Medical Review*), year XX, Series ii, No. 1, Krakow, 1964; and (b) the transcript of the testimony of Dr. Karolina Lanskoronska. They will be discussed later, after a more thorough discussion of the report of the Soviet Extraordinary State Commission.

Report of the Extraordinary Soviet State Commission

Some of the documentary evidence submitted to the Nuremberg Tribunal has been mentioned and discussed previously. At this point, I want to focus more closely on the contents of the report of the Soviet Extraordinary Commission. The Commission was created by the Soviet Government, purportedly to establish the extent of German war crimes in the Lviv region. It prepared a detailed report entitled *Protocol No. 47* and submitted it to the Military Tribunal in Nuremberg. The report was registered in the Acts of World War II War Crimes as RG 238-Ukrainian SSR-6. The Extraordinary Commission determined that the Germans had committed crimes against Soviet citizens when they occupied Lviv on June 30, 1941, and that a special group had been formed to establish a network of camps for the purpose of perpetrating mass-murder. The Extraordinary Commission determined that the chief organizer of the Nazi system for the mass destruction of human beings was Reichsminister Heinrich Himmler. Himmler came to Lviv soon after its occupation by the Germans to inspect and evaluate the efficiency of the "death camps," which had been set up on his orders in accordance with his plans.

During the course of its investigation, the Extraordinary Soviet State Commission had empowered a special local commission to investigate and establish the crimes which had been committed in Lviv and its environs in 1941. After completing its investigation, the special local commission submitted its report, entitled *Lviv Proofs*, to the Extraordinary Commission.

The special local commission was composed of: Major General I. Grushetsky, N. Kozyrev and W. Sadovy - members of the Supreme Soviet of the USSR; Dr. Trehub and E. Hrushko - members of the Lviv City Commission, P. Boiko - chairman of the Lviv City Commission; Turchenko, A.Vyshnevsky, S. Kuzmin - representing the Extraordinary State Commission; Dr. Avdyeyev - Chief of the Forensic Medicine Commission of the Red Army and his deputy,

Pukhnarevich; Golayev - forensic medicine expert; Gerasimov – criminology expert; Kortensov - prosecutor for the Lviv region; and Pizhanovsky - chief criminal investigator for the Lviv region.

The **Extraordinary Commission's** published report concluded with the following statement:

> On the basis of the evidence reviewed, this Extraordinary Commission has established that the German invaders murdered close to 700,000 Soviet citizens. Victims included men, women, and children in Lviv, Rava Ruska, Zolochiv, Sokal, Yavoriv, Zhovkiv, Horodky, Brody, Pidkamin, Nov-Yarycheve, Stanislav, and other areas of the Lviv region, as well as citizens of Czechoslovakia, Yugoslavia, the Netherlands, England, and the United States, who were brought to Lviv from concentration camps in Germany.

The Commission purportedly investigated not only the war crimes committed in Lviv, but in much of Galicia as well. The first part of the Commission's report was entitled "Execution of Distinguished Academics." Since that part of the report directly relates to allegations made against the Nachtigall Battalion many years later, I want to quote some additional passages from it:

> Even before it entered Lviv, the Gestapo had compiled lists of leading academicians who were to be executed, lists which had been ordered by the German government. Mass arrests and shootings began from the moment the Germans entered Lviv.

> The Gestapo arrested: Professor Tadeusz Boj-Zelenski, a member of the Association of Soviet Writers and author of many works; Professor Roman Renski of the Medical Institute; Volodymyr Seradsky, Rector and Professor of Criminal

Medicine at the Institute; Roman Longchamps de Berier, Professor of Law, along with his three sons; Professor Tadeusz Ostrowski; Professor Jan Grek; Professor Henryk Gilarowicz, surgeon; Professor-Stomalogist, Anton Cesenski; Witold Nowicki, Professor of Pathological Anatomy; Wlodzimierz Stozek and Anton Lomnicki, Professors of Mathematics at the Polytechnical School; academician Solovy; Kazimierz Bartel, an honorary faculty member of several universities; Stanislaw Pilat, Director of the Chemistry Department; Kasper Weigle, Roman Witkewycz, and Wladimierz Krukowski, Department Heads at the Polytechnical School; Professor Stanislaw Progulski; Professor Mendzewski; Adam Fischer, Ethnographer; well-known lawyer and member of the Polish State Codification Committee, Professor Mauricio Arenganda; Lviv writer Halyna Hlinska; critic Ostap Ortwina; university lecturers Auerbach and Riasecki; physicist Wander; engineer Simon Blumenthal; surgeon Ruffa; Docent Czortower; and other professors and lecturers of local institutions of higher learning.

Trampling on the human dignity of the academics, the Germans resorted to the most brutal methods of torture before shooting them. Golzman, a resident of Lviv, told the Extraordinary Commission that in July 1941, he saw 20 individuals, among them four professors, lawyers, and doctors being led into the courtyard of a building on Arziszewska Street, No. 8:

I knew one of them by name, Kreps, a Doctor of Law. There were five or six women in the group. The SS men forced all of these arrested individuals to clean all of the stairs in the fourteen-story building, using their mouths and tongues. When the stairs had been 'cleaned,' the SS forced the unfortunate individuals to pick up the trash in the courtyard, using the same method. All of the trash had to be placed into one designated pile. The custodian, of the building at No.8 Arziszewska Street, saw all of this too. Once the work was finished, the Gestapo selected five individuals from the group, took them out of the city, and shot them.

The fascist occupiers carefully covered up their tracks after killing the academics. The Germans refused to speak with any of the family members or friends who had come to ask about the fate of the arrested individuals. The Germans invariably answered all inquiries by stating, 'We have no information.' In the fall of 1943, by order of Reichsminister Himmler, members of the Gestapo burned the bodies of the Polish professors who had been shot in July 1941.

Mandel and Korn, who had been prisoners in the German camp on Janowska Street, were ordered by the Gestapo to dig up the bodies. They testified before the Extraordinary Commission, as follows:

> During the night of October 5, 1943, we were ordered by a member of the Gestapo to dig a hole between Kadet and Wulecka Streets. We dug the hole in the beams of light produced by lighting projectors, retrieved the thirty-six bodies buried there, and then we burned them all. While removing the bodies from the hole, we found several documents belonging to Professors Ostrowski, Stozek, the Head of the Department of Physical Mathematics at the University, and Kazimierz Bartel of the Polytechnic Institute.

Upon completion of its inquiry, the Extraordinary Commission determined that "...during the first several months of their occupation of Lviv, the Germans had arrested and murdered more than seventy of the most prominent academics in the fields of science and the arts." The report went on to list various categories of crimes which had been committed in the region. It also contained the testimony of many witnesses. The report listed names of the individuals who, it contended, were responsible for these crimes. The list of individuals accused by the Soviets of having committed war crimes in the Lviv region did not contain a single Ukrainian surname, let alone the name of any member of the Nachtigall Battalion. The vast majority of surnames were German. A few appeared to be Polish or Russian in origin. Nor did the list contain the name of Theodor Oberlander, the Nachtigall Battalion's German Liaison Officer, whom the Soviets suddenly began accusing of war crimes in 1959.

The Soviet Extraordinary Commission concluded its report as follows:

> The Extraordinary State Commission holds the Hitlerite Government responsible for the mass murder of civilian Soviet citizens, prisoners of war, and citizens of other countries, in Lviv and its environs. In particular, it blames Reichsminister Heinrich Himmler, who came to Lviv to supervise the German torturers and murderers. The following chief organizers and planners of the destruction of so many innocent people are also guilty... Every one of them bears great responsibility and should be severely punished and sentenced to lengthy prison terms.

The author has no doubt that the Soviet Extraordinary Commission exerted considerable effort to find a Ukrainian "bourgeois nationalist" to include on the list. This, of course, would have been helpful in discrediting Ukrainian nationalists, who were continuing their struggle against the Soviets at the very time that the Commission was engaged in its investigation.

It is important to reemphasize that there was no suggestion in the Soviet report that the German Army or the Nachtigall Battalion had committed any war crimes in Lviv in July 1941. The very fact that the Nachtigall Battalion was not mentioned in the Soviet Commission's report speaks volumes. Nor was there any allegation in the report that the Ukrainian Police or Ukrainian nationalists committed any war crimes or participated in any pogroms against the Jews. This fact is also very telling, inasmuch as some years later the Soviets and their allies suddenly began accusing Ukrainian nationalists of collaborating with the Nazis in the destruction of Jews. Similar accusations continue to surface from today's Kremlin and its controlled media, as well as some in the West, on a fairly regular basis.

The fact is that the Ukrainian Police was organized for the express purpose of maintaining public order, preventing looting, preventing destruction of property, and preventing anti-Jewish pogroms. The real Ukrainian Police, i.e., that which was under Ukrainian supervision (during the very short period of time that the Interim Ukrainian Government functioned) was strictly forbidden to engage in anti-Jewish pogroms and criminal acts against any civilians.

In his political memoir, *30-te chervnya, 1941* (30 of June 1941), **Yaroslav Stetsko**, the Premier of the Interim Ukrainian Government in Lviv, specifically addressed his government's position concerning the duties of the Ukrainian Police:

> Having a clear-cut position regarding the necessity of organizing our own police force…we immediately took steps to do so. June 30, Ivan Ravlyk was given responsibility of organizing a police force, which was to safeguard proceedings at the Prosvita Building. He was authorized to appoint a Chief of Police for the city of Lviv…Ivan Ravlyk

70

also accepted responsibility for organizing a Ukrainian militia in the entire region. He was instructed to issue orders immediately, in order to prevent any pogroms in the city which might be carried out by members of the criminal element, eager to take advantage of every chaotic situation.

It was for this very reason that local militia posts were to be opened, as soon as possible, in various parts of the city. Leaders of criminal gangs, who might begin to loot and steal under the pretext of participating in anti-Jewish demonstrations, provocateurs, thieves, and pogromists of every kind and nationality were to be dealt with summarily. Order was to be maintained with an iron hand. I remember clearly that the German SD and the Gestapo would appear in every city as soon as it was occupied and brought under control by the German army.

Ivan Ravlyk, and later Yevhen Vretsyona, performed their duties admirably. They prevented any anti-Jewish pogroms by Lviv's residents, maintained order, and helped save a number of Polish intellectuals. They would warn the Poles if they knew that the Gestapo was searching for them. Ivan Ravlyk, the organizer of the Ukrainian Police, died a martyr's death at the hands of the Gestapo, after undergoing months of torture. He was arrested in December 1941, together with his wife, his mother-in-law, and three other members of his family. His wife, mother-in-law, and the three family members were all shot by the Germans before Ravlyk himself succumbed. Earlier that same year, the Soviet NKVD had arrested Ravlyk's father, father-in-law, and sister, and exiled them to prison camps in Siberia.

One of the allegations made by the Gestapo against Ravlyk, in fact, was that he had refused to participate in actions against the Polish and Jewish populations of eastern Galicia. During his first two months of imprisonment he was repeatedly asked for lists of names and addresses of prominent Poles and Jews. He consistently refused to provide such information. Stepan Bandera and I whole-heartedly supported his steadfast refusal to cooperate with the Gestapo. We learned of it during our confinement in Berlin, prior to our formal arrest on September 15, 1941. Ivan Ravlyk's noble character - he was a revolutionary of the highest moral caliber - earned him the gratitude of the Polish and Jewish residents of Lviv.

This brief excerpt establishes the proper attitude of the Interim Ukrainian Government, whose members were also members of the OUN-B. The police, which was under its authority and supervision, was under specific orders from the leaders of the Interim Government to refrain from any acts of abuse or violence against Polish, Jewish and other citizens. The Ukrainian Nachtigall Battalion, which had been created by the OUN-B and whose members had sworn to support the Interim Ukrainian Government, was bound by the same directives.

Evidence gathered by Dr. Zygmunt Albert

The second important body of evidence which exists to help us evaluate the claims belatedly leveled by the Soviets and their allies against the Nachtigall Battalion, is a lengthy article published by Dr. Zygmunt Albert in *Przeglod Lekarski* (*Medical Review*), No. 1, 1964, entitled "The 25 Murdered Professors of Higher Institutions of Learning in Lwow Murdered by the Hitlerites in July 1941." Relying on the testimony of eyewitnesses, Albert described the murders in ..."Lekarski Widzial w Czasie Okupaciji Hitlerowskej 1941-1944" ("The Lwow Medical Society during the Hitlerite Occupation of 1941-1944"). His systematic entries in a diary during the occupation made it much easier for Albert to write his article. With the help of the diary he was able to recall specific events, the identities of specific individuals, and the contents of conversations with others. Also, Albert had access to several documents concerning the events of July 1941.

Dr. Albert remembered coming home from work on July 4, to find out that "special Hitlerite police units" had arrested 23 Polish professors and docents, some along with their families or co-tenants. All of them were shot within hours of their arrest, on the Wulecki Hills. The only one not shot was Professor Groger. Dr. Albert pointed to the directives of the German Government and the Governor, Hans Frank, to show that Nazi policy was to destroy the educated classes of the Eastern European occupied countries. The remaining population of *Untermenschen* would be allowed to obtain only an elementary education or lower-level trade skills, sufficient enough to enable them to perform the assigned tasks of serving the Germans.

On September 6, 1939, the Nazis arrested one hundred and eighty-three University of Krakow professors and docents. These academics had been "invited" to attend a conference at the Collegium Novum for the supposed purpose of hearing a lecture by Gestapo Sturmbannfuhrer, Dr. Bruno Miller. His lecture was titled "The Position of National Socialism on Education." After the lecture, all of the professors and docents were immediately arrested and transported to concentration camps in Germany, where most of them perished.

In the introduction to his article in *Przeglod Lekarski*, Dr. Albert wrote that he consciously began gathering evidence to establish the Nazis' murders of the Polish professors on the same day that he learned of them July 4, 1941. Albert hadn't realized until then that civilized Germans were capable of murdering innocent people. At times, he wrote, the collection and evaluation of the evidence was extremely burdensome, difficult, and certainly depressing. **Dr.Albert wrote further:**

> Articles concerning the executions of the Lwow professors had appeared in the Polish and foreign press. All of them, however, contained factual errors which, I think, I have been able to correct or explain.
>
> The liquidation of the professors began around 11:00 a.m. on July 2, with the arrest of Professor Kazimierz Bartel. His wife, Maria, stated: 'As everyone had to be at his place of work, my husband, who had a broken femur, went to the Polytechnical Institute on crutches. Shortly thereafter, three members of the Gestapo arrived at our home and asked for my husband. I told them that he had gone to the Institute. They took our daughter and instructed me to go to the Polytechnical Institute...'
>
> ...When Professor Nowicki was being arrested and saying goodbye to his wife, he whispered to her: 'We shall never see each other again.' Crying, his wife pleaded with the Gestapo for permission to give her husband a towel and some soap and was

told: 'He won't be needing them...'

...on the morning of July 4, we received news of the arrest of several other professors. The arrests had begun at ten o'clock the previous evening. Several groups consisting of one or two Gestapo officers, one or two non-commissioned Gestapo officers, or members of the field gendarmerie, spread out across the city by car. They broke into the homes of the Polish professors, whose names and addresses had already been compiled for them... The Gestapo had orders to arrest not only the professors whose names appeared on the list, but also to arrest all males over the age of 18 who might be found at the professors' homes.

The wife of Professor Henrik Gilarowicz stated: 'The arrest occurred close to 11:00 p.m. Seven uniformed members of the Gestapo burst into our home and fanned out into every room. Professor Wlodimierz Stozek was arrested by six Gestapo men'.

Continuing his description of the circumstances surrounding the arrest of each of the Polish professors, Dr. Albert emphasized that in every instance the arrest was made by the Gestapo. There was not one instance of an arrest made by a member of the Army, a member of the Nachtigall Battalion, or a member of the Ukrainian Police.

According to Dr. Albert, **Professor Ostrowski's daughter** stated that:

...from the moment the Gestapo burst into our apartment they behaved very rudely and brutally, prompting my mother to say, 'Bandits', to which one of the Gestapo men turned to her and barked in

Polish, 'Shut your mouth.' During the arrest of Professor Groger, one of the Gestapo men, learning that the professor's wife was English, began speaking to her in English.

Anela, wife of Professor R. Longchamps, recalled:

> All of them were in German uniforms. Four of them had SS markings on their uniforms and Death Heads on their hats. The others were in field uniforms and carried rifles. They spread out through the entire house. All of them spoke in German, and they had a list of names of fathers and sons, with their dates of birth.

According to the statements of several of the witnesses interviewed by Albert and quoted in his article, some of the Gestapo men spoke languages other than German. The Gestapo officer who barked at Mrs. Ostrowski in Polish was probably a *Volksdeutscher,* an ethnic German who was born and raised in Galicia. Many of these people fled from Galicia in 1939, when it was occupied by Soviet troops pursuant to the Molotov-Ribbentrop accord. In Germany, many such *Volksdeutscher* joined the police, the gendarmerie, or the Gestapo, and later returned to Eastern Europe as part of the German occupying forces.

Dr. Albert quoted at length from the statement of Professor Groger, the only one to survive among the Polish professors arrested. The day after his release, when asked by Albert what had happened in the Abramowicz Dormitory, Groger simply answered: 'It was something terrible…' Later, he would describe everything in great detail. Inasmuch as Professor Groger's eyewitness testimony as one of the Polish academics arrested has great significance, I will include his complete statement to Albert:

> We were driven to the Abramowicz Dormitory.
> The motor vehicle drove into the courtyard. We

were herded into the building and made to stand in the corridor, facing the wall. There were many professors already there. We were ordered to keep our heads down. If anyone dared to move, he was beaten over the head with fists or clubs. One time, when a new group of arrestees was brought into the building, I tried moving my head in order to look who they were and was hit hard on the head. I never tried to look again. It was about 12:30 a.m. and I continued standing, more or less motionless, until two o'clock. In the meantime, more individuals were being brought in and made to stand next to us. Every ten minutes or so, we heard screams and muffled shots from the basement of the building. After each shot, one of the German guards would say: *'Einer weniger'* (one less). I assumed then that he's saying this only to frighten us. Every few minutes someone's name was called out, and the individual was ordered to go to a room on the left.

I remember hearing Professor Ostrowski being ordered to go to the room and then heard my name being called out, as the tenth or twelfth individual. I found myself in a room with two officers. The one who had arrested me was young, and the second officer, obviously of higher rank, was very tall and heavily built. The latter shouted at me: 'You dog, you're a German, but you betrayed the Fatherland! You served the Bolsheviks! Why didn't you leave and go back to Germany with all of the other Germans?' I started to answer him, in a normal tone of voice. As he continued to shout at me, more and more loudly, I shouted back 'yes, I am of German extraction, but I consider myself a Pole. Indeed, even if I had wanted to go to back to Germany, the Soviets would never have given me permission to leave, because of my position in the community and their need for my services.'

The officers found business cards of several English Consulate members in my possession and asked me why I had them. I explained that my wife was English, and that we frequently entertained members of the English Consulate in our home. Toward the end of the interrogation, the senior officer began speaking more calmly and said, 'I have to speak with my chief. We'll see what we can do for you.'

He then left the room. The younger officer, who had arrested me, said quietly: 'It all depends on him. He has no superiors here. Tell him that you have made an important discovery in medicine which will be beneficial for the army. Maybe that will help you.' At that moment, the senior officer came back and simply ordered me to leave the room. I had no time to say anything else.

I was directed to the opposite side of the corridor and allowed to sit down and have a cigarette. I was even offered a glass of water. Professors Soloviy and Rentski were both standing near me. One of the Gestapo men asked them what their ages were, to which they responded seventy-three and seventy-six, respectively. I was sure that they would be released in view of their age.

I started to feel that my situation was looking better. The next minute, the senior officer told me to go into the courtyard and start walking around, adding: 'Behave as if you're not under arrest.' I began walking around the courtyard, smoking cigarette after cigarette and keeping my hands in my pockets. Another long minute went by. Suddenly, two Gestapo men entered the courtyard from the street. When they saw me, they ran up to me and one of them struck me in the face, screaming and demanding to know why I was loitering in the courtyard, with hands in my pockets. I explained that I had been ordered to do so, and to act as if I had not been arrested. They both mumbled something under their noses, apparently losing their interest in me, and proceeded to enter the building.

It was about 4:00 a.m. when a group of fifteen to twenty professors were led out of the building. In the lead were four men carrying the bloodied body of young Riffa. He was being carried by professors Nowicki, Pilat, Ostrowski and, I think, Stozek. They were quickly followed by Witkewicz. After the group walked past the gate into Abramowicz Street and disappeared from my sight, the Gestapo ordered Mrs. Ostrowska, Mrs. Grekow, and Mrs. Riffa to clean-up the blood on the stairs.

After another twenty minutes or so, I heard shots from the direction of the Wulecki Hills. Soon after, a new group of twenty or thirty individuals entered through the back entrance of the building and were ordered to stand in two rows, facing the walls of the corridor. Among them, I recognized Docent Mowczewski.

A little later, the Ostrowskis' and Grekows' domestic servants and the Ostrowskis' English teacher were led out of the building. The senior officer who had interrogated me asked them whether they were in fact the servants. The teacher pointedly demurred, and proudly declared that she was a teacher. The officer then ordered her to join the group standing against the wall and addressed his colleague loudly: those who were standing against the wall, he said, would be going to prison, but the servants would be freed.

Professor Bartel was arrested July 2, one day before the arrests of the other professors. He was being held in a small room on the ground floor of the Gestapo headquarters on Pelczynska Street. The Professor was allowed food parcels from home, which was his only source of food while in custody of the Gestapo. He was also allowed to write to his family and to receive mail from them.

In his letter of July16, written in German like all his letters, Professor Bartel wrote that he had not yet been interrogated. He understood that his only offense was that he had been the Polish Prime Minister who, allegedly, had negotiated with Stalin. In his letters he reported that the German officers and guards had dealt politely with him. In his letter of July 19, he listed the names of ten professors and asked what had happened to them. His letter of that day also requested that his correspondents 'wrap parcels for me in the latest Ukrainian newspapers, which should contain the most current information of interest to us here...'

In the letter dated July 20, Bartel expressed concern over news that his family had been evicted from their apartment. Anthony Stefanowicz, who had lived with the Bartels, and who was being held in custody with Professor Bartel, testified that at first the Germans behaved politely with the Professor. Later, after their transfer to the prison on Lonzka Street, the Germans' behavior towards Bartel worsened day-by-day. The Germans accused Bartel of maintaining contacts with Jews, and called him a 'slave of the Judeo-Communists.'

Stefanowicz stated: 'I remember very well, that toward the end of July or beginning of August, the Germans took the Professor out early one morning. They did not even let him put on his shoes or jacket, which seemed ominous to me. In fact, the Professor never did return, and his things were soon removed from the cell. Apparently, Professor Bartel was never interrogated, as he never mentioned it...'

Mrs. Bartel recalled: '...When the guards refused to accept the food parcel for my husband, I went to the office of the Commandant of the prison, Michaels, to inquire. The Commandant pointed to a dispatch in front of him and told me that my husband had been shot earlier that morning, on orders of Himmler. To my question, 'For what?' the Commandant replied: 'Because he was a leading Polish Communist.' Mrs. Bartel continued: 'He showed me the dispatch, but I was so shocked by the news of my husband's death that I was unable to comprehend its contents. I don't really remember whether I read it and forgot its contents or whether I never actually read it. I only saw my husband's name and Himmler's signature. The Polish prison guard told me simply: 'They took several of them out last night, including your husband.'

As we see from Professor Groger's statement, there is no suggestion that the Polish professors were arrested, interrogated, abused or murdered by members of the Nachtigall Battalion. There is no mention of Ukrainians, and no allegation claiming participation by the Ukrainian Police.

Concerning those responsible for the murders of the Polish professors in Lviv in the summer of 1941,
Dr. Zygmunt Albert concluded:

> Who committed those horrible, totally inexcusable, murders - Germans or Ukrainians? Among some Poles there continues to exist a belief that the acts were committed by Ukrainians. But doesn't everyone realize that under the Nazis nothing was done without orders from above? It is simply inconceivable to think that Ukrainians, especially those in German service, would have made the decision to arrest and execute a large number of prominent individuals in a city occupied by German military and civilian authorities.

The Statements of Countess Karolina Lanskoronska

In 1948, *Orzel Bialy* (*White Eagle*) a Polish émigré newspaper in London, England, published an article by Countess Karolina Lanskoronska entitled "The Germans in Lwow." In it she named the parties responsible for the murders of the Polish professors in Lviv, as well as members of the Polish intelligentsia in the city of Stanislaviv (now Ivano-Frankivsk). Dr. Karolina Lanskoronska was a Docent at the University of Lviv before World War II and had been directed by the Polish Committee in Krakow to establish a branch of the Committee in the "District of Galicia". She was arrested in the spring of 1942 in the city of Stanislaviv on orders of the chief of Gestapo, Hauptsturmfuhrer Hans Krieger. A year earlier, he had ordered the arrest and execution of 250 doctors, engineers and lecturers in Stanislaviv. During his interrogation of Lanskoronska, Krieger, perhaps certain that she would not be released, bragged to her about his participation in the murders of the Polish professors in Lviv and admitted that it was his doing.

He claimed, according to Lanskoronska, that the Field Gestapo had lists of individuals who were to be executed as soon as the Gestapo entered a newly occupied territory.

Krieger ordered the arrest and execution of the Polish professors in Lviv and later members of the Polish intelligentsia in Stanislaviv, whose names also appeared on prepared lists. The Field Gestapo did not stay long in any one area and moved forward along the front lines. It worked closely with the Einsatskommando SS, carrying out its orders: to arrest and execute every member of the Polish intelligentsia whose name appeared on the list.

On July 8, 1942, after five weeks in the Stalislaviv prison, Karolina Lanskoronska was transferred to the prison on Lonztki Street in Lviv. In Lviv, she was interrogated at the Gestapo Headquarters on Pelczynska Street by Walter Kutschmann, Commissar of Political Affairs. He told her that her Italian relatives (apparently members of the nobility) had interceded with Himmler on her behalf and had obtained authorization for her transfer to a prison in Lviv, over the objection of Hans Krieger. Sensing that Kutschmann did not like Krieger, she told Kutschmann about her two-month ordeal with Krieger. She spoke about the hunger and the darkness in her cell; she spoke about the ongoing sounds of executions in the basement and the mental torture of being led repeatedly to her own "execution", only to be given a reprieve at the last moment. She spoke about the brutal treatment of Poles in Stanislaviv and the arrests and disappearances of members of the city's intelligentsia. Kutschmann listened to Lanskoronska attentively and then got up. Clenching his teeth, he walked around the room and declared, "Krieger has other terrible things on his conscience as well, here in Lviv."

It was then that Lanskoronska decided to tell Kutschmann everything that she knew about Krieger. "I know that Krieger executed the professors of the University of Lviv, because he admitted to it to me on May 13, 1942." To this, Kutschmann responded, "I was with him then. I served under him." After her interrogation by Kutschmann, Lanskoronska was transferred to Berlin and from there to the concentration camp at Ravensbruck. On April 5, 1945, thanks to the efforts of her friend C. Burkhardt, Director of the International Red Cross in Geneva, she was freed and allowed to go to Switzerland. Krieger was removed from his post as chief of the Gestapo in Stanislaviv, in August 1942. He was prosecuted on Kutschmann's complaint, convicted, and sentenced to serve one year in prison for "revealing state secrets." In 1943, Krieger, now in the much-lower rank of *Untersturmfuhrer*, was transferred to France. He finished the war in Holland, where the British authorities released him from detention for lack of evidence, and then settled near Munster, Westphalia. There, in 1967, Krieger became one of the main defendants in war crimes proceedings against former members of the SS for the killings in Stanislaviv during the war. The court, however, found insufficient evidence to prove his guilt for the killings, concluding that his boasts to Lanskoronska may have simply been an effort to frighten her.

Considering the findings of the Soviet Extraordinary State Commission, the statements of the witnesses cited by Dr. Zygmunt Albert and his conclusions, and the statements of Karolina Lanskoronska, it becomes manifestly clear that the Nachtigall Battalion had no involvement whatsoever in the arrests or murders of the Polish professors in Lviv during the summer of 1941. This is further corroborated by the previously-cited testimony of the Commander of the First Battalion of Brandenburg Corps D.o.D 800, under whom the Nachtigall Battalion had been placed during the German advance eastward.

The following facts constitute additional proof that the murders of the Polish professors were committed by the Germans: In October 1943, the Germans decided to rebury the bodies of the Polish professors who had been murdered in 1941. A brigade of Jewish prisoners, dispatched to the area where the graves were thought to be located, was unable to find them. A Gestapo officer summoned to the scene, however, was able to point to the location of the graves immediately. The burial sites of the Polish professors, like those of other Nazi victims, were well-known to the Gestapo.

The Nachtigall Battalion was stationed in Lviv from the early morning hours of June 30 through July 5, 1941. As a member of the Battalion, I solemnly declare that during that time neither I, nor any member of the Battalion, was ever involved in the arrest, abuse, mistreatment, torture or death of any Polish academic in Lviv, nor the abuse or death of any Jewish resident of the city. I also declare that during our Battalion's brief stay in Lviv, I did not see any dead bodies on the streets of the city, or any bodies hanging from lamp posts or balconies. Nor did I see any "rivers of blood," which supposed researchers of the events of that tragic time period (Dmytruk, Galski, Danylenko, Polishchuk, Friedman, Wilczur, Prus and Korman) have alleged in their publications.

Executions of Jewish Residents of Lviv, 1941

With the end of the Second World War, one of the Soviet Government's most important goals was to divert the hatred of the Poles away from the new Communist regime and toward Ukrainian "nationalists." The Soviets retained the services of several Jewish, Polish and Ukrainian "historians", including A. Auerbach, F. Friedman, M. Herder, A. Korman, S. Krakowski, S. Polishchuk, E. Prus, H. Wasser, and J. Wilczur, for assistance with their anti-Ukrainian campaign.

Thus began the creation, evolution, and widespread distribution of a myriad of anti-Ukrainian legends. The shelves of bookstores in the Soviet Union, Poland and other countries were soon filled with works by "historians" in the Kremlin's pay, full of mendacious

anti-Ukrainian drivel. The Soviets were eagerly assisted in their anti-Ukrainian propaganda campaign by their allies, the East

Germans and the Polish Communists. Following reunification of East and West Germany, even some German "historians" joined the effort to create enmity between Ukrainians, Jews, and Poles. In various newspapers and magazine articles, books, and during many academic conferences, many German historians went so far as to suggest that Ukrainians exceeded the Nazis in their barbarity toward the Jews! According to some of them, the Holocaust began in Lviv during the first week of July 1941. This viewpoint even appeared in a U. S. Senate Proclamation sponsored by Senator Charles Percy of Illinois, adopted on April 23, 1983.

While I have no intention of disputing the widely-accepted number of victims of the Holocaust, it is interesting to note how the number of alleged Jewish victims in Lviv during the first days of July, 1941, fluctuated from report to report. In its May 1942, report to the British Government concerning the persecution of Polish Jews, the Jewish Bund in Warsaw claimed that, "…30,000 Jews have been killed in Lwow." Toward the end of 1942, in a book entitled *The Black Book of Polish Jewry,* Eleanor Roosevelt, wife of President Franklin D. Roosevelt, and co-author Albert Einstein, the world-famous physicist, alleged that 50,000 Jews had been killed in Lviv in 1941. In the British Parliament, Lord Selborn, Minister of the Exchequer, put the figure of Jews murdered in Lviv at close to 400,000! As we can clearly see, the number of alleged Jewish victims in Lviv grew from day-to-day, to an outlandishly improbably high figure. The entire population of Lviv at that time was less than 400,000.

Eventually, the number of Jews alleged to have perished in Lviv in July 1941, dropped precipitously. In January 1945, for example, J. Silberstein of Geneva, Switzerland, an eyewitness writing in a French publication, estimated the number of Jewish victims in Lviv to be 15,000. In 1946, historian F. Friedman of Lodz, Poland, also claiming to be an eyewitness to the events, put the number of Jewish victims in Lviv at 7,000. Somewhat more recently, in 1990, the *Encyclopedia of the Holocaust,* published in Jerusalem, claimed that, "Ukrainians from neighboring villages, using knives and axes, murdered 2,000 Jews in Lviv during July 1941." The encyclopedia named this period "Days of Petlura." (Editor's note: It is inconceivable that Ukrainians in western Ukraine would have referred to July 1941, as the "Days of Petlura," as Petlura was not a popular political figure in western Ukraine. In fact, he was considered a traitor by many for having "betrayed" Galician Ukrainians in the Polish-Ukrainian Treaty of 1921, pursuant to which Poland was awarded eastern Galicia in exchange for its help in clearing central and eastern Ukraine of Bolshevik troops.) Interestingly, no photographs have been found showing "Ukrainian peasants armed with knives and axes..." murdering Jews in Lviv, as alleged in the encyclopedia. As I have stated before, I spent June 30 and the first five days of July 1941, marching or walking along many of Lviv's streets, and did not see a single body hanging from a balcony or lamp post, contrary to what some authors have alleged. Now, let us turn to some other sources and documents which never seem to be mentioned by those who have vilified the Nachtigall Battalion. Those sources and documents present a version which is very different from the one advanced by the Soviets and their erstwhile bedfellows concerning those terrible, early days of July 1941, in Lviv.

Dr. Moritz Allerhand prepared a report concerning events in Lviv from June 30, 1941, through March 1, 1942, which he submitted to the Polish underground and which can be considered authoritative. In his report, we read that the Germans were abusing Jews on July 1, 1941, during anti-Jewish "actions." Dr. Allerhand claimed that one person "apparently" had been killed. According to his report, the anti-Jewish actions lasted for several hours and ended at 3:00 p.m. To the best of my knowledge, Dr. Allerhand's report has never been published and remains under "lock and key" at the Jewish Institute in Warsaw.

Let us also consider the August 15, 1941, dispatch of Rowecki, a commander of the Polish AK, the *Armiya Krajowa* (Home Army), to the Polish Government-in-exile in London. Rowecki's report claimed that, "...there were no murders of Jews in Lwow at the time of its initial occupation by the Germans."

Major "Vyetyer" (Yevhen Berezhnyak) was the commander of a group of Soviet intelligence officers who were ordered to stay behind when the Red Army evacuated Lviv. He reported that, "...the Banderites were already shooting at soldiers of the Red Army and at civilians from basements and rooftops on June 22, 1941..." But Yevhen Berezhnyak's group didn't witness any mass killings of Jews and did not characterize the period as the "Days of Petlura," as some purported eyewitnesses have done. It is also interesting to note that the enterprising Major placed the "Banderites" in Lviv on June 22, 1941, a full week before the German Army and the Nachtigall Battalion entered Lviv.

In November 1941, the *Daily Bulletin of the Jewish Telegraphic Agency* in New York City reported the following from Lviv: "Notwithstanding the efforts of occupying German authorities to agitate the Ukrainians against Jews, the Ukrainian leadership in Galicia has been cooperating with local Jewish leaders, with whom they had been cooperating during the years of the Polish regime.

Local Ukrainians, who have been entrusted with the civil administration, have been demonstrating an understanding of the Jewish dilemma and have been trying to make life for Jews easier, to the extent they can." This report, I submit, truthfully and accurately characterizes the behavior of the vast majority of the Ukrainian population of Lviv toward their Jewish neighbors in 1941. And this was not the only such report. *The Jewish Telegraphic Agency* reported in similar fashion about the situation in Galicia and Ukraine eight times during 1941.

One need not be an historian to realize from the documentary evidence just mentioned that the various accusations which have been leveled against Ukrainians, and Ukrainian "nationalists" in particular, have the clear earmarks of malicious defamation typical of Soviet political propaganda. All archival institutions in the Soviet Union were under the strict control of the NKVD, the Soviet internal secret police. Soviet archivists were given an important assignment, which was to search the archives for "enemies of the people", that is, opponents of the Soviet regime, and to look for any documents or other materials which could be used to defame them.

While the Soviet archives were supposedly reorganized and the procedures revised in 1958, the "organs" (the MVD, later the KGB) continued to supervise the administration of the archives until the dissolution of the Soviet Union. The Soviet-era archives remain the exclusive purview of the successor security police in today's Russia, the FSB.

Recently, over 400 valuable documents have been stolen from the Historical Archives in Lviv. Investigators believe that a sophisticated plan was developed to accomplish the theft of the documents. "The archives contained materials dealing with the heritage of the Ukrainian nation and the heritage of our national minorities," said Dr. Yaroslav Dashkevych. "In Lviv, Ukrainians and Jews enjoyed good relations. For some reason, documents which described that relationship have disappeared." (http://www.maidan.org.ua/ static/mai/1125140931.html).

Soviet practices over the course of seventy years included the wholesale destruction or concealment of documentary and other evidence which might point to crimes committed by the Soviets. The Soviets consistently and shamelessly put the blame for those crimes on others. As was previously noted, only recently has the Russian Government finally admitted that the murders of some 7,000 Polish army officers in Katyn Forest, near Smolensk, Russia, were committed by the Soviet NKVD, not by the Germans.

The "Oberlander Affair" and Allegations Against the Nachtigall Battalion

After Stalin's death, the Soviet Union's satellites in Eastern Europe experienced a gradual process of national revival. The 1953 revolt of the workers in East Berlin shook the Soviet Bloc to its core. Three hundred thousand workers walked off their job sites. For the next three weeks they occupied or closed factories, broke open prisons, and blocked Soviet tanks which were sent to squelch their demonstrations. News of the workers' actions in Berlin spread across the rest of East Germany, and similar workers' strikes occurred in other major cities of the country. Massive work stoppages and demonstrations took place in Leipzig, Magdeburg, Dresden, and other cities.

The workers' strikes were eventually suppressed by brutal force according to the Communists' traditional methods of dealing with "malcontents." Dismissing the idea of negotiating with striking workers (whom the communists claimed they represented), the East German authorities ordered motorized army divisions against them. The army mercilessly crushed the striking East German workers, using machine guns, grenades, cannons, and tanks. Similar upheavals occurred in Poland. In 1949, Yugoslavia refused to continue following Moscow's directives, and Romania also began following a more independent policy. Then came the stormy year of 1956, when workers' strikes brought Poland and Hungary to a standstill.

It was then that leaders in the Kremlin concluded that they could no longer count on the ability of the communist regimes in Eastern Europe to maintain control in their countries, nor on their loyalty to Moscow. Primary responsibility for crushing the revolution in Hungary was given to Yurii Andropov, then the Soviet ambassador in Budapest. Andropov would later become the "liberal" leader of the Soviet Union. He was very successful in completing his no-nonsense assignment and, in return, was well rewarded. He was recalled to Moscow in 1957 and placed in charge of the Directorate, the office responsible for maintaining relations with Communist Parties in the Soviet Bloc countries. In his new role, Andropov traveled widely and conducted frequent meetings with the communist leaders of the satellite states. His task was to make sure that they maintained order and domestic stability and, of course, closely followed Moscow's directives. He seemed to be successful in his newest assignment as well.

In Ukraine, which had suffered tremendously during the Second World War, a spirit of freedom was also being reborn during Khrushchev's "thaw". Ukrainians eagerly began reading the patriotic poetry of the Shestydesyatnyky (writers of the 1960s). This talented and charismatic group of young writers and poets began asserting individual human rights and the rights of all nations, boldly rejecting the Communist Party's insistence that artists create their work with the government-approved style of "Socialist Realism." The people's aspiration for freedom slowly began to chip away at their deep-seated fear of the Soviet regime. Even the labor camps in the Soviet GULAG began experiencing more frequent strikes by inmates.

West Germany was very effectively healing its wounds from the war. With generous aid from the United States, West German Chancellor Konrad Adenauer was well on his way to rebuilding the country and transforming it into the economic powerhouse of Europe and an equal partner in the Western community. NATO, which included West Germany as one of its founding member states, had become an important military alliance, able to effectively defend western Europe in the event of a Soviet attack.

The Soviet leadership apparently concluded that it had to react to these developments and do so quickly. Among other things, it decided to embarrass Chancellor Adenauer and, hopefully, bring down his government. Andropov had established a large network of agents in the satellite countries for purposes of espionage and diversionary activity. Again he was given a new assignment: to develop a plan to embarrass, destabilize, and bring down the government of Konrad Adenauer.

In the early 1950s, Theodor Oberlander was beginning his career in West German politics. His political base included millions of German refugees who had been forcibly evicted from their ancestral homes in Prussia, Silesia, and other lands and forced to settle in West Germany after the war. Understandably, many of them held strongly anti-communist views. Oberlander was himself a strong anti-communist and was popular among the refugees. He began organizing an anti-communist political party in West Germany which presented an ideological threat to the Soviets. In 1953, he was named by Konrad Adenauer to head the Ministry responsible for German political refugees and victims of the war. Oberlander's work in the ministry quickly attracted the attention of the Soviet leadership, on whose orders NKVD searched Soviet and East German files. Among the cache of German wartime documents, they discovered evidence that Oberlander had briefly commanded a battalion of Ukrainian nationalist soldiers in 1941: the Nachtigall Battalion. Furthermore, how very convenient that the Battalion had been among the first to enter Lviv, remaining there for the first week of the German occupation of the city!

Why not put the blame for the thousands of dead left by the NKVD in the jails and prisons of Lviv on Oberlander and the Nachtigall Battalion? Furthermore, why not blame Oberlander and the Nachtigall Battalion for the arrests and murders of the Polish professors and Jews in Lviv during the July 1941, atrocities which had been committed primarily by the Einsatzgruppen? Why not blame all of the crimes which had occurred in Lviv on Oberlander and "his Ukrainian Battalion"? By doing so, the Soviets would be able kill several birds with one stone, as it were. By implicating Oberlander in the crimes, which had been committed in Lviv by the NKVD, the Einsatzgruppen and the Gestapo, the Soviets could seriously embarrass and undermine the West German Government, suggesting that it was full of Nazi war criminals. At the same time, it would enable the Soviets to paint Ukrainian nationalists as

Nazis. Prosecutors had made the same accusations against Ukrainian nationalists during the Nuremberg proceedings, but they had been unable to convince the tribunal of the validity of their claim. The Nuremberg Tribunal cleared the "Ukrainian nationalists" of responsibility for any war crime, but this was no impediment to the Soviets in 1959. They confidently launched their latest propaganda blitz, knowing that they could establish their allegations against Oberlander and the Nachtigall Battalion in "court proceedings" which they would control. The anti-Oberlander, anti-Nachtigall project was quickly formulated, approved, and put into action.

The NKVD began its work earnestly in the fall of 1959. Helpful "witnesses" were quickly tracked down, briefed, and their testimony recorded. Reporters from the newspapers, radio and television were invited to interview "witnesses" in various countries and report their new revelations. In the span of a single month, the Soviets quickly and efficiently discovered "new" evidence, and arranged for the publication of a book entitled *The Truth about Oberlander,* subtitled *The Brown Book.* Its publisher, a communist-front organization named "The Committee for German Unity," loudly trumpeted the "new" discovery of a West German Cabinet Minister's criminal Nazi past!

One wonders why the Soviets searched for witnesses from around the globe but did not search harder for more witnesses who had been actual residents of Lviv during July 1941. Surely, there must have been many witnesses still living in Lviv who could remember the first days of the German occupation. But those witnesses would probably remember the thousands of mutilated bodies which had been left in the prisons by the NKVD on the eve of the German occupation of the city. Obviously, that would not be helpful for what the Soviets had in mind: the defamation of Theodor Oberlander and the Nachtigall Battalion, and the embarrassment and downfall of the West German Government.

The testimonies appearing in the *Brown Book* were gathered by the Soviets between October 10 and November 5, 1959. Such a quick, efficient collection of testimony speaks for itself. In any case, the testimony of nineteen alleged eyewitnesses was quickly collected. Witnesses suddenly and vividly remembered specific events which had occurred and positively identified faces which they had supposedly seen from afar, almost two decades earlier. Why had it taken so long to discover Oberlander's alleged criminal past? And how were the Soviets and East Germans able to collect so much evidence in a single month, evidence which had not been "discovered" for almost twenty years?

With great fanfare the witnesses' statements were released to the public. One witness was interviewed on East German radio, two witnesses were interviewed on East German television, and four were interviewed by members of the official Soviet press. To collect the testimony of the various witnesses, East German correspondents had been sent to Israel, Warsaw and Lviv. They managed to find only three witnesses in Lviv. The other witnesses, found in Israel, Poland and Germany stated that they happened to be in Lviv at the time of the German occupation in 1941.

At a press conference held on October 22, 1959, the Committee for German Unity accused Oberlander of being one of the most prominent Nazi "warmongers" and advocates of mass killings. The Committee alleged that: Oberlander had stood with Hitler in opposition to the Weimar Republic; that he had occupied the highest positions in the SA, the Nazi Party, and other Nazi organizations; and that he had advocated the destruction of mankind undertaken by the Nazi leadership. It alleged that, as a member of German military intelligence, he had stirred up members of the minority German ethnic populations (the fifth column) in countries of Eastern Europe. In this manner, he helped to orchestrate the war. Additionally, the Committee alleged that as commander of a "special fascist military unit," he was responsible for Nazi atrocities and killings in Lviv and other Ukrainian cities, and that he participated in the murder of members of the intelligentsia in Czechoslovakia.

The **Committee for German Unity** concluded:

> Such criminals from the fascist past should be brought to justice and deprived of the right to occupy any government position. The citizens of West Germany demand that war criminals like Oberlander be removed from office as ministers in the government and from parliament, and that they be tried in a court of law as war criminals.

The **Committee for German Unity** (Berlin, B-8-169/70 Friedrichstrasse) claimed to be acting "on behalf of the good name of the citizens of Germany." It released the alleged documentary evidence concerning Oberlander to the public in February 1960. The materials contained a great deal of inherently suspect testimony concerning the organization and execution of killings in Lviv. The Committee's book included a distorted and ideologically slanted biography of Oberlander and discussed his activities from the time that he became Director of the Institute of East European Refugee Settlement in the late 1930s to 1959. Then, it set forth the testimonies of nineteen purported witnesses which, it claimed, established and proved that:

1. The Nachtigall Battalion occupied Lviv on June 29, 1941, and immediately started pogroms against the Jews and Poles.

2. Two days later on July 1, 1941, arrests and executions began, including the arrests and murders of thirty-four Polish professors, whose names appeared on lists which had been prepared in Krakow by Oberlander and Bandera.

3. Oberlander and the Nachtigall Battalion remained in Lviv for seven days, during which time five thousand people were murdered by the Battalion and units of the SS and SD that arrived later in the week.

4. The SS and SD were assisted by the Militia, which was composed of Ukrainian fascists, led by soldiers of the Nachtigall Battalion.

5. The Committee claimed that Oberlander was responsible for the organization of the Nachtigall Battalion from among "Ukrainian fascists and hooligans", whose job it was to attack the Soviet rear guard, to commit acts of sabotage, and to instigate and conduct pogroms. The Committee also claimed that, as the organizer and commander of the Nachtigall Battalion, Oberlander was fully responsible for the criminal acts which the Battalion had commited. Furthermore, the Committee for German Unity alleged that members of the Nachtigall Battalion, trained and led by Oberlander, became especially known for their cruelty. Later they formed the core of the Ukrainian SS Galizien Division, which "... murdered millions of Soviet citizens: Jews, Poles, and other non-Aryans."

Having quickly collected their alleged evidence and "testimony" of witnesses, the Communists immediately began loudly publicizing them in advance of the "court proceedings", which would take place, conveniently, in an East German court in East Berlin. Later, judicially-ordered inquiries would also be conducted in West Germany.

Court Proceedings in East Germany

In the history of jurisprudence, rarely has there been a criminal case involving the same individual, the same allegations, and the same evidence which resulted in diametrically opposed conclusions. The first tribunal, in communist East Germany, predictably found Oberlander guilty *in absentia* and sentenced him to death. The second proceeding, a prosecutorial inquiry in West Germany, would conclude that there was no credible evidence to substantiate the charges against either Obelander or the Nachtigall Battalion. How can one account for such diametrically opposed results? This can be explained only by the fact that judicial systems in East Germany, the Soviet Union, and other Communist and totalitarian countries differed (and continue to differ) markedly from the judicial systems in West Germany and in other democratic countries.

In the former East Germany, as in the former Soviet Union, all laws were enacted for the express purpose of assuring the continuing, unchallenged, and absolute supremacy and control by the Communist Party of the State. In the Soviet Union and its satellite states, of which East Germany was perhaps the most loyal and doctrinaire, the judicial authorities were an integral part of the ruling Communist Party establishment. They were instructed by higher authorities at the beginning of any case involving political or ideological issues (and most likely, instinctively knew even without receiving specific instructions) what their decision and the outcome of the trial must be. The decision of the court was invariably preordained.

In the Soviet Union and other totalitarian communist (and non-communist) countries, being labeled an opponent of the "system" rendered an accused automatically guilty of whatever charge might be brought against him by the authorities. The judicial proceedings that followed were a mere formality. The Oberlander case was a classic example of the way in which truth and justice were immaterial considerations for the court, whose sole duty was to follow the dictates and maintain the authority and control of the Communist Party and State.

At least four questions concerning proceedings against Oberlander and the Nachtigall Battalion in East Germany should be asked:

1. Why did the East German authorities wait for almost twenty years before filing charges against Oberlander?

2. Why were the government's witnesses primarily individuals who had never lived in Lviv, where the claimed atrocities had been committed? How could they be more knowledgeable and more credible than actual residents of the city?

3. Why had the supposed witnesses not reported the atrocities which they had witnessed to the Soviets during the Soviet commission's investigation in 1944?

4. Why were proceedings conducted in East Germany, and not in Lviv, in the Soviet Union, where the defendants had allegedly committed the crimes with which they were charged ?

In his publication *Zvynuvachuyu* (*I Accuse*), B. P. Byelayev claimed that, as soon as the Germans had evacuated Lviv in 1944, he was flown to the city for the purpose of beginning an investigation of German war crimes. Wouldn't he have looked for witnesses among the city's residents as an essential part of his investigation? Wouldn't he have come upon the witnesses who would later testify in the East German court proceeding?

The East German court's introductory comments at beginning of the "trial" read, in part, as follows:

Adenauer continues to stand behind Oberlander, even after the press conference held by the Committee for German Unity on October 23, 1959. Drawing on original documents, this conference established that Minister Oberlander was one of the leading instigators of the Fascist war and one of the proponents of the policy of mass murder. Adenauer continues to defend Oberlander, even after the publication of *The Brown Book-The Truth about Oberlander*, which contains documentary evidence demonstrating Oberlander's guilt.

How can one support a government whose leader (Adenauer) has kept silent about the war crimes of a cabinet minister about which he has known for at least seven years? What kind of government hides such criminals and continues to give a minister its full confidence... in face of irrefutable proofs of the minister's guilt?

The court's introduction contained additional accusations:

The behavior of the Adenauer government is characteristic of a purely militaristic system, whose purpose is the continued obfuscation of the fascist past, inasmuch as the government intends to launch a new war of aggression. To do so, the system requires the services of those old soldiers who have led Germany to catastrophe twice before. With their assistance, the government in Bonn wants to provoke a third massacre of nations, this time using atomic weapons.

These two short excerpts from the East German tribunal's introductory comments are more than enough to show that the proceedings were being conducted primarily for political reasons, and that the issue of the guilt or innocence of the individual accused was of purely secondary nature. Court proceedings in Lviv would have been much less effective in terms of propaganda value than proceedings in East Germany, next door to West Germany. Furthermore, proceedings in Lviv would have opened the door to the unpleasant possibility of local witnesses bringing up matters concerning the murders perpetrated by Soviet NKVD there, in June 1941.

The fierce press and media campaign against Oberlander and the ensuing "court proceedings" in East Berlin ended, predictably, with a determination of Oberlander's guilt and a sentence of death. In an attempt to get even more propaganda "mileage" from the proceedings, the East Germans later reduced Oberlander's sentence to life imprisonment, to show the "leniency" of the communist judicial system.

Accusations Against the Nachtigall Battalion in the East German Court

The principal accusations leveled against the Nachtigall Battalion by the East Germans, acting as surrogates for the Soviets, were the following:

> ...the Nachtigall Battalion was organized from among Ukrainian terrorists and chauvinists of Bandera. Oberlander, the Battalion's military commander, trained the Battalion in the spirit of service to the ideology of fascism, hatred of communism, anti-Semitism, and readiness to murder the intelligentsia of Eastern Europe.

> Taking advantage of his many years of service as an officer in military intelligence, and assigned to a sabotage unit within the Central Military Command, Oberlander trained members of the Nachtigall Battalion for the purpose of preparing diversionary actions, performing acts of sabotage, and carrying out pogroms and shootings. Command of the Nachtigall Battalion was placed in the hands of Oberlander, who was one of the most dangerous German officers. When the Battalion attacked the Soviet university city of Lviv in the early morning hours of June 30, 1941, its members immediately began pogroms against the Jews and a systematic destruction of the city's intelligentsia, using lists which had been prepared in advance.

Testimony of witnesses in the East German court proceedings was supposed to prove the participation of the Nachtigall Battalion in crimes committed during the first days of the German occupation of the city of Lviv. What did the witnesses testify to?

Witness Spidal testified about the supposed "special military training" of the Nachtigall Battalion at the Ukrainian camp in Brandenburg, Germany. In fact, such a camp never existed. He also testified that he had been assigned to the Battalion on the second or third day of the German occupation of Lviv, and he saw civilians being executed by the Germans and members of the Nachtigall Battalion.

Another witness, Melnyk, testified that he first heard the name Oberlander when he was "heading toward Lviv." He claimed that members of the Nachtigall Battalion told him on June 30, 1941, that their commanders, Shukhevych and Oberlander, had provided them with lists containing names of individuals whom they were to arrest and execute. Later, they allegedly boasted to him that they had done so. Query: why was Melnyk traveling to Lviv, and how was he able to meet and gain the confidence of the members of the Battalion so quickly? Why would they admit to any such "death lists" to a stranger, and boast about committing these executions on June 30, their first day in Lviv? It has been established clearly that the shootings began on July 2 and 3. The testimony of the first two witnesses raises immediate doubts about their credibility.

Yet another witness, a woman named Kukhar, testified that in the early morning hours on July 7 (the same day that the Nachtigall Battalion left Lviv), while looking out from her second story balcony, she saw people being shot in the street by a group of officers. She claimed that the face of one of the officers whom she had seen in the street had stayed in her memory since that day, and that she immediately recognized him as the man who had "looked into my window" when his photograph was shown to her in 1959. Is it possible to distinguish so easily the face of a soldier in uniform, standing at a distance, and immediately recognize him in a photograph almost twenty years later?

Witness Maurice Reiss testified that he first learned from Mrs. S. Sicher, after moving to Israel, that the Germans had posted notices with the name Nachtigall printed on them, with orders to the residents of the city of Lviv. Interestingly, he testified that he had never seen such notices while he was in Lviv.

Theodore Sulim testified that shootings and tortures began as soon as the Germans and the Nachtigall Battalion entered Lviv. According to his testimony, bodies were strewn in the streets and hung from balconies. Twelve people were hung from the balcony of the Opera Theatre, among them his friend from the city of Kolomyya, Serhij Hlibovych.

Witness Fritz Hibner, a German, testified that he arrived in Lviv with a group which was assigned to secure the city's main buildings. He claimed that he saw soldiers leading civilians down the street and then saw the soldiers shoot them. The executions were witnessed by a group of officers. Hibner was able to identify Oberlander as one of the officers from a photograph in a newspaper in 1959. Another witness, Pankiw, testified that his friend had told him that Oberlander had played a major role in the killings of the Polish academicians.

All of the other witnesses testified in general about the atrocities committed by the Germans. Witness Sokolnicki testified, at length, about the murdered Polish professors but did not claim that they had been killed by members of the Nachtigall Battalion. Other witnesses produced and were permitted to give hearsay testimony, such as: "others said...we heard...everybody knew..." that the Germans were assisted in making their arrests and conducting the executions by the "fascist Banderite bands" of the Nachtigall Battalion. Witness Gorczak, for example, testified that "...one woman, who had good contacts and acquaintances among the Germans, learned who had planned the arrests and murders and gave me their names. They were the following: General of the SS, Katzman and Gestapo thugs Grzymek, Rokita, Piontek, Blum and Gebauer. And, she added, the most important man in the group was Oberlander. However, she was unable to give any details about him."

Perhaps the most inventive testimony was that of Mrs. Szkurpello-

Weisner. She claimed that "…on the day when the German army occupied Lwow, I was returning home from the store where I worked at the time. Walking home, I saw groups of Ukrainian fascists in their unique hats, coming into the city on horseback."

Mrs. Weisner added:

> I lived just a few meters from the Brygidka prison and know for certain that a few days before abandoning Lwow, prior to the German occupation, the Soviets had released all of the prisoners. Later, notices were posted directing Ukrainians and Poles to go to the city's prisons to identify the bodies of their murdered relatives. I never heard of even one individual identifying a relative. The bodies had already decomposed as they had been exposed to the sun for several days. The residents claimed that the dead were victims of the Soviets. But the prisons had been emptied by the time the Germans arrived. So how could these have been victims of the Soviets? Many people later realized that the identification of victims was simply choreographed by the Germans in order to cast blame onto the Soviets.

It is transparently obvious that Mrs. Weisner's testimony, claiming that the Soviets had released their prisoners before abandoning Lviv, was dictated to her by the Soviets, whose usual practice rarely included releasing political prisoners slated for execution.

None of witnesses produced by the Soviets testified that he or she personally observed anyone from the Nachtigall Battalion, or even anyone from the local Ukrainian Police, committing a criminal offense against a particular individual, on a particular day, at a particular time. All of the purported witnesses' statements were inherently incredible, vague, conclusory, or based entirely on hearsay.

Decision of the East German Court

The court proceedings in East Germany followed established Soviet and Communist practices. Neither the prosecution nor the defense examined the charges and the defense material in any meaningful way. With regard to the charges against the Nachtigall Battalion, "defense counsel" stipulated that members of the Battalion, as well as other members of the OUN-B, had been authorized by the Germans to commit criminal acts against civilians. The defense conceded the prosecution's allegations that the Nachtigall Battalion had "committed crimes", arguing only that the Battalion had no part in planning the war. The defense never investigated the witnesses or their backgrounds to determine whether they had personal knowledge of the events to which they testified in court, or whether they had any reason or motive to testify in the manner they did. The defense didn't even cross-examine the witnesses effectively in court to test their recollection and credibility.

The East German court's finding, comprised of 19 pages, dealt mostly with the minor discrepancies between the prosecution and defense, and it was full of political hyperbole and ideologically charged language. The court's decision was, of course, preordained. After issuing a verdict of guilty against Theodor Oberlander and the Nachtigall Battalion for murder and the incitement of others to murder, the **East German Court stated**:

> With the coming of Hitler to power, the accused took part in the preparation and execution of Germany's imperialist aggression during the Second World War. The criminal acts of the accused were the fruits of German politics of imperialism and militarism. German imperialism spread terror and destruction and covered the earth in blood in both World Wars.

The court mischaracterized Oberlander's activities since 1945. It accused him of involvement with several "reactionary" organizations and with conducting a "policy fraught with danger for peace in Europe and the world." "By his actions," the court declared, "he has proven that he has no intention of ceasing the same kind of criminal activity that he committed during the time of German fascism. He is fully responsible for those crimes and cannot be morally excused." Somewhat over-dramatically, the East German court even credited Theodor Oberlander with playing a dominant role in planning the war. He had, it said, instigated the war against Poland.

The court demanded that Oberlander's immunity from criminal prosecution (as a member of the West German Bundestag) be lifted, and that he be prosecuted for his crimes in West Germany. In accordance with the precedent established by the Nuremberg Military Tribunal, the East German Court sentenced Oberlander to death. Later, it reduced the sentence to life in prison.

The East German legal system was based on the judicial system existing in the Soviet Union. The theoretical basis for this system was explained by Andrej Vyshinsky in a treatise, which enjoyed great popularity in the Soviet Union for many years. Vyshinsky, who had been the prosecutor during the Stalinist "show trials" in the late 1930s, was the principal Soviet prosecutor at the Nuremberg proceedings. Later, he would be named as the Soviet Union's representative to the United Nations. In Vyshinsky's view, Soviet law was intended to serve a single primary purpose: to protect and defend the interests and needs of the Soviet State and the ruling Communist Party. Its obligation was to make sure that the current leadership of the Communist Party maintained absolute control over the country's citizens. Soviet law was not intended to protect individual citizens or groups from abuse by governmental or party officials. Soviet and East German jurisprudence and criminal law were essentially identical. In both systems, the accused was always presumed guilty and could never rely on the impartiality or objectivity of the court.

It may be helpful to quote a few words from Nikita Khrushchev, leader of the Soviet Union during the late 1950s and early 1960s, regarding trials held against real or imagined opponents of the Soviet regime during the Stalinist years. Writing about the trial of Kossior, a long-time loyal Communist Party member who suddenly fell out of favor with Stalin, Khrushchev recalled:

> Judge Rodos was an individual without intelligence and a creature devoid of any morality. How could such an individual conduct a trial against Kossior or anyone else? During a meeting of the Presidium of the Central Committee, we questioned him about some conflicting matters. Rodos told us: 'I was told that Kossior and Chubar were enemies of the people and that I, as the judge who was to question them, was expected to obtain their confession, that they indeed were enemies of the people.'

Of course, Khrushchev's comments were completely disingenuous, as it is impossible to believe that he or any other high-ranking Soviet leader could have been surprised by Rodos' admissions. "Show trials" had been going on for decades in Soviet Russia. Who can reasonably doubt that the testimony of the incriminating witnesses in the Oberlander-Nachtigall proceedings was obtained in similar ways? Testimony was extracted by any number of methods regularly employed by the Soviets: the use or threat of imprisonment, torture, loss of employment, reprisals against family and relatives, or perhaps simply material or other inducements.

The Communists also accused Theodor Oberlander and the Nachtigall Battalion of the very crimes which they had committed before abandoning the city of Lviv in late June 1941. They intentionally disseminated false accusations, assuming that people would believe them. The court proceeding in East Germany was simply an exercise in political propaganda, and its judicial decision was rendered despite the complete lack of credible evidence against the defendants.

The Nachtigall Battalion in West German Legal Proceedings

Under a continuing "propaganda barrage" from East Germany regarding Theodor Oberlander, one of its own ministers, the West German government of Chancellor Adenauer decided that it could not ignore the very serious charges and must conduct its own inquiry. In the West German Federal Republic, the collection of evidence against Nazis and war criminals was gathered by the Vereinigung der Vervolgten der Nazi-regims (The Association of Victims of Nazism), more commonly known as VVN, whose main office was in Ludwigsburg. The VVN transmitted evidence which it gathered (more accurately, which it received from the East Germans or Soviets), to prosecuting officials in West Germany. The VVN would invariably repeat the allegations against Oberlander and the Nachtigall Battalion which appeared in the Soviet and East German press. Parroting the East Germans and the Soviets, the VVN alleged that the Nachtigall Battalion, acting under direct orders from Theodor Oberlander, had murdered a group of Polish academics and 3,000 Jews in Lviv. Similar deeds were committed by the Battalion in the towns of Zolochiv, Sataniv, Yuzvyn and Mikhalpole.

Not surprisingly, the VVN's complaint made no mention of the fact that the Soviet Extraordinary Commission had investigated war crimes during the German occupation of Lviv in July 1941, determining that the crimes in Lviv and in other cities of eastern Galicia had been committed by the Germans. The commission's findings had been confirmed by the Nuremberg Tribunal.

Fortunately, the West Germans did not accept the evidence submitted by the VVN and began their own independent investigation. The West German investigation of the allegations against Theodor Oberlander and the Nachtigall Battalion was assigned to the prosecutor for the district court of Bonn, the capital of West Germany. The investigation and trial of Theodor Oberlander and the Nachtigall Battalion in the court of Soviet-occupied East Germany was one thing. The court-ordered investigation conducted by the West German prosecutor was something entirely different. The prosecutor in Bonn conducted a detailed review of the allegations against Oberlander and the Nachtigall Battalion, interviewed many eyewitnesses and examined many documents. He found no credible evidence to support the specific allegations made against Theodor Oberlander and the Nachtigall Battalion. The judicially-ordered prosecutorial investigation in West Germany determined that the residents of Lviv first discovered the bodies of thousands of murdered inmates in the city's prisons on June 28, 1941. This was two days before the German Army and the Nachtigall Battalion entered the city.

The prosecutorial investigation concluded that the first German forces to enter Lviv were members of the First Mountain Division, soldiers of regiments 98 and 99, artillery regiments 79 and 111 of the Mountain Division, as well as advance groups of the 68th Infantry Division, selected members of the 258th Battalion, the advance group of the 53rd artillery regiment, and the Nachtigall Battalion. The Germans first heard of the massive killings when they approached the outskirts of Lviv. Great numbers of the city's residents, whom they met on the streets, told them about the bodies in the prisons. The commanders of the individual units, as well as the field command which was established, gave orders to move the bodies from the city's three prisons into the prison courtyards. The bodies were laid out in the courtyards to facilitate identification by relatives, and then were buried in a common grave. Some of the bodies were so badly decomposed that identification was impossible. The number of corpses found in the prisons of Lviv exceeded three thousand. Among them were the bodies of four German pilots who had been captured by the Soviets.

The witnesses in the West German proceedings who testified to the atrocities found in the prisons of Lviv in June 1941, were mostly former soldiers of the German army units which had entered the city on June 30. Many of them had taken photographs, which they presented to the court. Their testimony was corroborated by the journals or diaries, which some had kept or by letters which some of them had written to families or friends. Their testimony established, unequivocally, that the murders of the prison inmates in Lviv had occurred prior to the German occupation of the city. Based on the evidence the prosecutorial authorities in Bonn received, considered, and reviewed, it was determined by the investigating prosecutor that:

1. Prior to the beginning of the Soviet-German war on June 22, 1941, the Soviets had arrested many people in Lviv who were considered to be opponents of the Soviet regime (mostly Ukrainian nationalists) and held them in the city's prisons;

2. When it proved impossible to remove the prisoners into the interior of the Soviet Union, the Central Committee of the Communist Party of the Soviet Union ordered that they be executed. The number of prisoners executed was determined to be in excess of 3,000, as determined by those in charge of disposing the bodies.

3. The executions occurred prior to the entry of German forces into the city.

The findings of the prosecutorial inquiry in West Germany refuted the false accusations made by the Soviets that the killings of civilians in the Lviv prisons had been committed by Germans after they occupied the city. The prosecutors considered and evaluated the sworn testimony of two groups of eyewitnesses, along with examining and reviewing various documentary evidence. The eyewitness testimony was provided by former soldiers who marched into Lviv with the German army and by lay witnesses who had been residents of the city at the time. The documentary evidence consisted of contemporaneous reports which had been prepared and filed by German Army officers who had participated in the occupation of Lviv.

Of particular interest was the testimony of an individual whose identity was not revealed for security reasons. The witness had been a Soviet citizen who had been sent to Lviv several months before the outbreak of the Soviet-German war. There he met and became friends with the local chief of the NKVD, whom he met again after the Germans were driven out. The NKVD chief told him that immediately after the outbreak of the Soviet-German war on June 22, 1941, a fresh wave of arrests was ordered by the Soviet authorities. Those arrested were mostly Ukrainians (thought to be anti-Soviet), whose names appeared on lists which had been prepared by the NKVD earlier. Because of the breakdown of transportation in western Ukraine, it was no longer possible for the Soviets to deport their prisoners to the interior of the Soviet Union. By the evening of June 23, 1941, the Germans were already within thirty kilometers of Lviv, and a decision was made by the top leadership in Moscow to execute all of the prisoners. The witness testified that the local NKVD chief told him (the witness) that he had received a telegram from NKVD Headquarters in Moscow instructing him to execute all of the prisoners being held by the NKVD in Lviv's prisons. The telegram was initialed "N.K" (Nikita Khrushchev?). The witness' testimony established that the murders of the prisoners were carried out by the local NKVD, on direct orders from the Kremlin.

With respect to allegations that soldiers of the Nachtigall Battalion had participated in the murder of Jews being held in the NKVD prisons, the West German prosecutor came to the following conclusion: "Prior to its entry into Lviv, a part of the Nachtigall Battalion received orders to occupy the prisons and release those prisoners who were still alive." The second company of the Battalion had orders to occupy the headquarters of the NKVD and the prison there. According to witness "G", he saw German soldiers there. The soldiers were apparently speaking in Ukrainian, however, which led the witness to assume that they were members of the Nachtigall Battalion. But knowledge of the Ukrainian language does not necessarily prove that the speakers were members of the Nachtigall Battalion, as the Germans recruited individuals who spoke the local language to the field gendarmerie. Besides, the Germans had interpreters who wore army uniforms. When witness "G" was shown photos displaying various German uniforms, he pointed to a photograph depicting a uniform with an armband on the sleeve, with the words "Deutsche Wehrmacht" sewn on it. Such armbands were worn only by the field police and *gendermarie*.

After considering the sworn testimony of many witnesses including evangelist pastor "M" (whose church was opposed to Nazi policies), former soldiers of the Wehrmacht, former members of the Nachtigall Battalion and their Chaplain Rev. Dr. Ivan Hrynyokh, and from extensive documentary evidence, the prosecutor concluded that:

1. The Nachtigall Battalion had never received an order or orders of any kind to abuse, mistreat, torture or kill Jews, Poles or other civilians.

2. Given the strict discipline in the Battalion, no member of the Battalion would have countenanced any such action on his own initiative.

3. There was no credible evidence that any unit or individual member of the Nachtigall Battalion had participated in the abuse, mistreatment, torture or killing of Jews, Poles or other civilians in Lviv, or any other city or town.

The investigating prosecutor, therefore, concluded that allegations leveled against Theodor Oberlander and the Nachtigall Battalion by the VVN were unsupported by any credible evidence. Accordingly, the prosecutor declined to initiate formal criminal prosecutions against Oberlander or any former member of the Nachtigall Battalion.

As a former member of the Nachtigall Battalion and a participant in the German occupation of Lviv between June 30 and July 6, 1941, I solemnly declare that at no time did our Battalion receive any authorization, order, or implicit suggestion from our commanding officers to abuse, beat, harass, injure, or otherwise mistreat or kill Jews, Poles or other civilians in Lviv. This holds true for all the other towns of Western Ukraine which we entered. Furthermore, I never heard of a single incident involving a member of our Battalion abusing civilians, including Jews and Poles. If such an incident had occurred, it would have been practically impossible for it to remain a secret among the close-knit members of our Battalion.

The investigation in West Germany included an inquiry into the activities of the Einsatzgruppen, which were among the first German units ordered by Heinrich Himmler to advance eastward behind the front lines. Their infamous activities had been thoroughly examined during the Nuremberg proceedings. The Einsatzgruppen which entered Lviv were commanded by Dr. Rasch. One unit of the group, numbering about 2,000 men and personally led by Rasch, entered Lviv at 5:00 a.m. on July 1, 1941. A second unit entered the city on the following day. After discovering the murdered prison inmates in the NKVD jails and reporting the gruesome discovery to his superiors, Rasch ordered his group to punish the Jews as being "co-responsible" for the murders. It is a tragic fact that innocent Jews were unjustly punished for the murders of the Ukrainian prison inmates which had been committed by the Soviet NKVD, but those "reprisal killings" were not the work of Ukrainian soldiers.

The West German prosecutor's investigation also determined conclusively that Stepan Bandera was not with the Nachtigall Battalion when it entered Lviv on June 30, 1941, as he was in German custody in Berlin. The prosecutor concluded that the assassination of Bandera had no relation to the proceedings concerning Theodor Oberlander. Rather, it was carried out on the orders of the Soviet Government. The prosecutor's investigation and findings illustrated, once again, the nefarious methods used by the Soviets in pursuing their policies and goals, the inseparable relationship between the political authorities and the courts in the Communist system, and the Communists' total and utter disregard for the truth.

The West German prosecutors concluded that the Einsatzgruppen were responsible for the murders of the Polish academicians and Jewish residents of Lviv and other Ukrainian cities and towns. The same determination had been made by the Nuremberg Tribunal. The West German investigation also determined that the Soviets had attempted to shift blame for the murder of the Ukrainian prison inmates to the Germans. The investigation likewise determined that the Soviets had committed the brutal murders of Lviv's Ukrainians shortly before the German occupation of the city, and that the Einsatzgruppen had committed similarly brutal crimes against the Jewish residents of the city shortly thereafter. Neither Theodor Oberlander nor the Nachtigall Battalion were found to be implicated in the murders of the Polish academicians and Jewish residents of the city. It should be noted that Theodor Oberlander, having been cleared of any wrongdoing by the Bonn prosecutor's investigation, sued those who had accused him of murder and war crimes for libel and slander and won successful verdicts against his accusers.

Defamation of Ukrainian Nationalists

"The Union of Soviet Socialist Republics is the most advanced country in the world!" We used to hear this and similar propagandistic claims quite often prior to 1991, the year the Soviet Union disintegrated. In certain aspects the claim was accurate. No other country could compete with the Soviet Union in the areas of ideological warfare, propaganda and disinformation.

"The proletariat cannot accept the existence and strengthening of nationalism. On the contrary, it supports everything which helps to erase national differences, erases national boundaries, and makes international bonds stronger." (Vladimir Lenin. *Works*. Volume 24, Page 129. Moscow.) Lenin's teachings were paraphrased by N. Wozniak, the author of a Soviet-inspired diatribe entitled *Yikh Spravzhye Oblycchya* (*Their True Face*). "Bourgeois propagandists pay unceasing attention to nationalism and religion. Both of those ideologies...play on the national and religious feelings of people and dull class consciousness. Nationalism is a disease. Once it infects someone, it can often reappear."

Religious belief and patriotism are the two great elements in the Ukrainian national character which the atheistic Soviet system was unable to destroy. These Ukrainian characteristics undoubtedly caused headaches for the Communist leaders in the Kremlin. In the 1970s, Ukrainians began speaking up courageously and demanding the national, political, and religious rights which were "guaranteed" to them by the very progressive-sounding Soviet Constitution. Many years had passed since the Second World War and the struggle of the OUN and the Ukrainian Insurgent Army against the Soviets. A new generation had grown up knowing little or nothing of that struggle. The Soviets always understood and feared the spirit of Ukrainian nationalism and the Ukrainians' deeply-held religious beliefs. Karl Marx, the ideologue of communism, derisively called religion "the opium of the people." The Soviets realized that the spirit of Ukrainian nationalism, their belief in God and respect for the spiritual and moral teachings of Christianity, were still very much alive and widespread among Ukrainians. Therefore, the head of the KGB Yurii Andropov ordered his subordinates to resume harsh treatment of all Ukrainian "nationalists" and religious practitioners. This had been a standard practice of the Soviets.

As part of the renewed anti-Ukrainian campaign, the Soviets resumed a new propaganda war. Almost immediately, the shelves of Soviet bookstores became filled with "new" books regurgitating standard Soviet invectives against Ukrainian patriots and religious believers. As always, the purpose was to defame the Ukrainians' long, heroic struggle for freedom and independence. But since that couldn't be accomplished by printing the truth, the authors had to rely on misrepresentations and lies. They portrayed Ukrainian freedom fighters as "bandits, thieves, murderers, traitors" and, naturally, as "enemies of the people."

Yaroslav Stetsko, Premier of the short-lived Interim Ukrainian Government in June-July of 1941, described the Soviet ideological campaign in the following words:

> Today, the Soviets (and their allies) are the only ones who equate the Ukrainian struggle for independence with the Nazis. They even suggest that Ukrainian nationalists served the Nazis, and that Stepan Bandera asked the Germans to put him in a concentration camp in order to give him an "aura" of a persecuted potical leader. This ludicrous claim originated with Dimitri Manuilsky, former foreign minister of the Ukrainian S.S.R., who first made it at a conference of teachers from the western regions of Ukraine, held in Lviv on January 6, 1945.

In *Pid Chuzhymy Praporamy* (*Under Foreign Flags*), Volodymyr Byelayev and Mykhailo Rudnytsky quoted at length from a Nazi document, a document well-known in the West, giving instructions to the German police. They intentionally omitted a very important sentence from the document: "Our enemies are communists, Banderites, and partisans. The most dangerous of them are the Banderites. They must be destroyed at any cost."

The *Litopys Ukrayinskoyi Povstanskoyi Armiyi* (Annals of the Ukrainian Insurgent Army), Vol. 9, characterizes the Soviet ideological and propaganda war against Ukrainians simply and clearly:

> The Soviets have been conducting an intensive ideological and propaganda campaign against all organizations and political parties advocating Ukrainian independence. Not having the ability to effectively challenge the legitimacy of the arguments in support of Ukrainian independence, the Soviets simply accuse the Ukrainian independence movement of collaborating with the Nazis. In particular, they regularly level such allegations against the OUN and the Ukrainian Insurgent Army (*UPA*). The truth is that the Ukrainian independence movement, the OUN, and the *UPA*, have always been guided solely by the interests of the Ukrainian people and have struggled heroically for the independence of Ukraine, whether or not that goal was acceptable to others.

The Soviet characterization of the activities of the OUN, *UPA*, and other Ukrainian patriotic organizations as "collaboration with foreign intelligence agencies" had several important, inextricably linked objectives: 1. create a myth that Ukrainian patriotic organizations "worked for German marks or American dollars," 2. sow suspicion and discord between the leadership of Ukrainian political organizations and their rank-and-file members, 3. disparage the Ukrainian independence movement as nothing more than a "an agent of foreign powers," 4. convince the

Ukrainian people, the membership of Ukrainian organizations and the international community, that the Ukrainian SSR, a constituent republic of the Soviet Union, was an independent, sovereign country, 5. disarm or neutralize opposition to Soviet rule and, if possible, destroy the Ukrainian independence movement, and 6. kill the aspirations of Ukrainians for their own independence, and eventually to undermine and ultimately destroy the consciousness of Ukrainians as a separate nation. Soviet policies and propaganda were not new or original and had their origins in Tsarist Russia. Soviet behavior, tactics, lies, and deceptions were inherited from the secret police of Tsarist Russia and simply adapted.

S. T. Danylenko, the author of *Doroha Han'by i Zrady* (*The Road of Shame and Treason*), resorted to outlandish lies when writing about the leadership of the Ukrainian independence movement. Following are a few examples of his inventiveness. On page 205 of *"Doroha…"* he wrote: "Stepan Bandera arrived in Lviv on June 30, 1941, incognito. His security service had reported that his opponents (followers of Andrii Melnyk), learning that Bandera had formed a Ukrainian government, decided to eliminate him and assigned the task to Senyk-Hrybiwsky." On page 236, Danylenko quoted Bandera purportedly stating: "These traitors (referring to members of the Melnyk faction of OUN) have violated the *Decalogue* of a Ukrainian Nationalist and deserve the death penalty." According to Danylenko, Bandera gave a list of names of various members of the Melnyk faction to the Gestapo, which carried out the sentences. Bandera and Stetsko, claimed Danylenko, got the Gestapo to eliminate many of their opponents.

On page 237, Danylenko even claimed that Bandera and Stetsko were not really inmates of the Sachsenhausen concentration camp during the duration of the war, but "…lived in comfortable villas." Still later, on page 246, he claimed that Roman Shukhevych was appointed commander of the Ukrainian Insurgent Army by none other than Heinrich Himmler, chief of the SS. This was a particularly fantastic claim, as the UPA fought its first battles against the Germans. UPA began its military activities against the Soviets only after the German retreat and the Soviet re-occupation of western Ukraine in 1944.

Danylenko also wrote a pamphlet attacking the Ukrainian Greek Catholic Church as a collaborator of the Nazi regime. The Ukrainian Greek Catholic Church had been officially liquidated by the Soviets in 1946 during a so-called Church Sobor (Council), called by the NKVD on Stalin's orders. The terrorized priests and laymen present at the Council dutifully voted to "self-liquidate" their church and join the Russian Orthodox Church. None of the Church's bishops were present for the vote, since all had been previously arrested by the NKVD. The Soviets would continuously pretend that the Ukrainian Greek Catholic Church had "voluntarily" joined the "Mother Church" (to which the Ukrainian Greek Catholic Church had never belonged).

Similarly ridiculous claims were made by another Soviet propagandist, Bohdan Vasylenko, in his pamphlet entitled *Lzhemesiyi* (*Messiahs of Lies*). On page 43 he wrote: "The so-called Transcarpathian Ukrainian Republic, with its Jesuit priest Voloshyn as president, and the 'independent Ukraine' proclaimed by Stetsko in Lviv, were pathetic farces, orchestrated and directed by the German fascists..." The author conveniently failed to mention, of course, that the Germans had permitted the Hungarians to overrun and annex the Transcarpathian Ukrainian Republic (1939). Furthermore, the Germans had promptly arrested the leaders of the interim Ukrainian Government, headed by Stetsko, when they refused to rescind their declaration of independence on June 30, 1941. Vasylenko also failed to mention that the Nazis began a reign of terror against Ukrainian nationalists in 1941, hunting down and murdering thousands of them, including many at Babyn Yar in Kyiv.

Yet another Soviet propagandist, Vitaliy Maslovsky, in his pamphlet *Zhovto-Blakytna Mafia* (*The Blue-and-Yellow Mafia*), claimed that Roman Shukhevych, "Hauptsturmfuhrer in the SS", was named commander of the Ukrainian Insurgent Army by Heinrich Himmler. Like Vasylenko before him, he conveniently forgot to mention that Shukhevych had never been a member of Himmler's SS. Maslovsky even claimed that the major conferences of the OUN were called by the Gestapo. And, for good measure, he also threw in the allegation that "...UPA began a bloody war against its own people..."

Major Galski "Klym Dmytruk"

Klym Dmytruk, still another Soviet propagandist, was the author of *Bezbatchenky* (*Bastards*), which was published in two editions, in 1972 and 1974. Who was Dmytruk? *Ukrayinskyj Visnyk* (*The Ukrainian Herald*), a popular underground publication in Soviet Ukraine, wrote the following about "Dmytruk":

> ... Klym Dmytruk is the pseudonym of KGB Major Klymentii Galski, the organizer and co-participant of a number of illegal, criminal acts... Klymentii Galski, a Pole by ethnicity, was born in Zhytomyr, Ukraine. He was about 45-50 years of age in 1945 and had served in the MVD-KGB since the Second World War. In 1944, he was working in the Radekhiv raiion (county) of the Lviv oblast (region), where he participated in many illegal activities against the civilian population suspected of sympathizing with the Ukrainian underground. He participated in similar illegal actions in other parts of Lviv Oblast. He took part in the fabrication of MVD-KGB cases against political defendants and in the execution of prisoners, and advanced quickly in the ranks of the Soviet secret police. Dmytruk/Galski was assigned to handle the most 'sensitive' cases, and took part in the preparation and

fabrication of cases against Yurii Shukhevych (1958), Levko Lukyanenko (1960), and the Ukrainian National Committee in Lviv (1961).

Yurii Shukhevych was the son of Roman Shukhevych, the political commander of the Nachtigall Battalion and later, the Supreme Commander of the Ukrainian Insurgent Army. Yurii was arrested in 1947 at the age of fifteen for being the son of an "enemy of the people." He was convicted and sentenced to 10 years in prison because he refused to condemn his father and his father's anti-Soviet activities. When Shukhevych was released early, a year and a half before completion of his sentence, the General Prosecutor of the Soviet Union, Rudenko, objected. So, Yurii was returned to the Vladimir prison to serve out the balance of his sentence.

Not long before his scheduled release date, Yurii Shukhevych was visited by none other than Major Galski. The major urged Shukhevych to condemn the activities of his now deceased father and the Ukrainian guerilla movement which he had led (Roman Shukhevych was killed in 1950 during an ambush by the Soviet NKVD, on the outskirts of Lviv). Yurii Shukhevych again refused to condemn his father or the movement to which he had devoted his life. Not surprisingly, on the day of Shukhevych's scheduled release, new charges were filed against him. This time he was charged with committing acts constituting "anti-Soviet propaganda and agitation." He was, of course, quickly convicted and sentenced to another 10-year prison term.

The new charges against Yurii Shukhevych were fabricated by Major Galski with the help of two degenerate stukachi (prisoners regularly used by Soviet prison authorities to engage their "political" cellmates in provocative conversations, in order to obtain evidence of "anti-Soviet crimes"). One of them, Alexander Fomenko, from the Moscow countryside, had been convicted of armed robbery in 1947 and sentenced to 25 years in prison. In 1951, he was sentenced to an additional 25 years for participating in an unauthorized organization, *Dvuglavyj Oryel* (The *Two-*

headed Eagle) in the prison camp. The second, Burkov, a Russian from Voronezh, had been sentenced to 10 years for slitting a victim's throat. Galski had obtained their cooperation and "services" rather cheaply. He promised them a transfer from prison to a prison camp, where they would, presumably, lead an easier existence. Thus, several days before Yurii Shukhevych's newest scheduled release, Burkov submitted a written "citizen's complaint" to the local prosecutor objecting to Shukhevych's release, alleging that Shukhevych had engaged in "anti-Soviet agitation" while in the cell with Fomenko and Burkov. On the basis of Burkov's "citizen's complaint", an official "investigation" was duly initiated and Shukhevych was taken to the NKVD's Lviv prison for interrogation. This new investigation was conducted by a Captain Vinogradov, who had earned a reputation for torturing prisoners during Stalin's years. Just prior to his interrogation of Shukhevych, Vinogradov had beaten women prisoners Zarytska, Husyak, and Didyk.

Shukhevych's trial was held in secret. Forgetting or confusing most of their previous statements, Fomenko and Burkov testified that Shukhevych spent most of his time in the prison cell studying foreign languages. Undeterred by this unexpected change in the testimony of his witnesses, the prosecutor simply argued that studying a foreign language constituted evidence of Shukhevych's intent to flee from the Soviet Union! Daring to leave the Soviet Union (the "Workers' Paradise") was, of course, also a very serious crime. Easily satisfied that studying foreign languages was proof of criminal intent, the court predictably entered a guilty verdict against Shukhevych.

When Galski met with Shukhevych again, he cynically admitted that the charges had been fabricated. He assured Shukhevych, however, that if he were to reconsider his stubborn position and begin cooperating with the NKVD/KGB, the verdict could easily be set aside. All that he had to do was to write an article denouncing Ukrainian nationalism and condemning his father's activities against the Soviets. This discussion occurred in

December 1958. Yurii Shukhevych again steadfastly refused Galski's offer and was promptly sentenced to another ten years in prison! Three years later, in 1961, Shukhevych was returned to Lviv, where he met with Major Galski again. And once again, Galski promised Shukhevych an early release from prison if he cooperated with the Soviet authorities' request.

People who have dealt with Major Galski have characterized him as a clever, devious individual. He was a complete cynic who never bothered to hide his intentions or thoughts when interrogating a prisoner. He was a passionate anti-Ukrainian from personal conviction, not simply because of his job. Galski used various approaches and techniques with those whom he interrogated. With some, he was polite, civil, and seemingly even friendly. With others, he was abusive and physically violent. Galski was particularily brutal toward Mykhailo Osadch, a Ukrainian journalist writer, during the latter's interrogation in 1965.

Klymentii Galski was eventually transferred from the KGB's regional office in Lviv to its "Ukrainian" headquarters in Kyiv. It became well-known that among his newer assignments was the surveillance and recruitment of Ukrainians living abroad who returned to Ukraine as tourists, businessmen or as representatives of Western governments or organizations. He was also placed in charge of the preparation and publication of political literature for Ukrainians living abroad. It was in this capacity that KGB Major Galski assumed the name of "Klym Dmytruk". As a Soviet propagandist, Galski-Dmytruk's assignment, like the assignment of other "writers," was to portray the Ukrainian independence movement as a "fascist" plan fully in complete sync with the Nazis, and dangerously hostile to the "peace-loving peoples of the Soviet Union." According to Galski, the real goal of the OUN and the Ukrainian Insurgent Army was to "enslave" the Ukrainian people by transforming Ukraine into a German colony, turning all Ukrainians into slave laborers!

127

Major Galski/Klym Dmytruk spared no invectives in his writings, not even against the clergy and hierarchy of the Ukrainian Greek Catholic Church, whom he also portrayed as active Nazi collaborators, except, of course, those who had "seen the light" and joined the Russian Orthodox Church. On page 191 of *Bezbatchenky (Bastards),* for example, Galski wrote the following: "The arrogant chaplain of the Nachtigall Battalion, Hrynyokh, dressed in his flashy new Wehrmacht uniform and surrounded by the ever-so ready-to-serve clerical staff at St. Yurii's Cathedral, lived comfortably in one of Metropolitan Sheptytsky's apartments…"

As supposed evidence of the Ukrainian Church's "collaboration" with the Germans, Galski/Klymuk quoted from a letter apparently sent to Metropolitan Sheptytsky by officers Yevhen Pobihushchy, Roman Shukhevych, Mykhailo Brygidyr, Vasyl Sydor, Pavlyk-Orlyk and Dr. Herman Holovatsky on March 13, 1942. It was sent from Frankfurt an der Oder, where the former members of the disbanded Nachtigall and Roland Battalions were completing their retraining as members of the new Schutmannschaftsbattalion-201.

Galski quoted the following passage as proof of his contention:

> Your Excellency! After several months of training here in Frankfurt, we are leaving for the Eastern Front to continue our fight against the Soviets. At this important time, we remember you, our spiritual Father. Not knowing what our fate will be and whether we will remain among the living, we ask for your Fatherly Blessing on the road ahead. We thank your Excellency for assigning a priest for our spiritual care.

A prideful atheist, **Galski cynically commented**:
And so, Sheptytsky again gave his blessing to the

Battalion of murderers to commit new crimes. The previous year...the same leaders, together with their chaplain, had come to Sheptytsky for his blessing. He granted Shukhevych and Hrynyokh an audience during which he listened closely to their reports. He gave his blessing to the members of the Nachtigall Battalion and to the future government which the Ukrainian nationalists planned to establish.

KGB Major Galski/Dmytruk surely must have had access to various documents concerning the crimes actually committed by the Nazis in Lviv, and certainly must have known about the report of the Soviet Extraordinary Commission, which had concluded that the crimes had been committed by the Germans. But, as it would clearly contradict his anti-Ukrainian claims, Galski/Dmytruk kept silent about the Commission and its findings.

"Danylenko" and "Belayev"

Author Danylenko's specific assignment was to impeach the Ukrainian Greek Catholic Church. The assignment was not an easy one. He had to expend considerable effort to write the 360 pages of his book, *Doroha Han'by i Zrady* (*The Road of Shame and Treason*), but demonstrated considerable talent in doing so. Danylenko's literary *oeuvre* was devoted entirely to shamelessly besmirching the reputation of Metropolitan Andrej Sheptytsky, the spiritual leader of the Ukrainian Greek Catholic Church from 1901 to 1944. In his "documentary publication", Danylenko portrayed Sheptytsky as an "enemy of the Ukrainian people" and a "...lackey of the Vatican, the Austrian Hapsburgs, and the Nazis." He even accused Sheptytsky of being a spy for the Nazis. Danylenko's considerable talents as an inventive writer of fiction produced a portrait of Metropolitan Sheptytsky as perhaps one of the twentieth century's greatest criminals!

Danylenko did not forget to mention the Nachtigall Battalion in his vicious diatribes against Metropolitan Sheptytsky. On page 200, for example, he alleged that the chain-of-command in the Ukrainian nationalist underground had issued the following order: "Instigate a revolt, beat, kill, burn, destroy! Not a single Soviet should remain alive!" Danylenko claimed that the Ukrainian nationalists beat and tortured Soviet officials and their families before killing them. "These bloody executions were carried out at Abramowicz dormitory by Oberlander, Shukhevych, and other members of the Ukrainian nationalist leadership, together with officers of the Abwehr-2 and the Gestapo." (Page 202.)

Writing about Sheptytsky's relationship with the Nachtigall Battalion and other Ukrainian nationalists, Danylenko came up with the following claim: "...the official, ceremonial audience with Metropolitan Sheptytsky came to an end. Chaplain Hrynyokh then asked the Metropolitan for permission to discuss pressing matters of state importance. Shukhevych, as the personal representative of Bandera, and Oberlander, as the representative of the German High Command, declared that '...today, or tomorrow at the latest, a Ukrainian government will be proclaimed.' They went on to say that Bandera, the leader of the OUN, wanted to confer with the Metropolitan. Sheptytsky agreed to meet with Bandera. A half-hour later, the Ukrainian nationalists brought Stepan Bandera to the Metropolitan's residence..." However, Danylenko did not explain how Bandera, who was then in German custody in Berlin, approximately 600 miles from Lviv, could have gotten to the cathedral in Lviv in thirty minutes.

The Nachtigall Battalion was given even more attention by "Belayev", another Soviet propagandist, who wrote a booklet entitled *Ya Zvynuvachuyu* (*I Accuse*). Who was Belayev? Unfortunately, we don't know.

On pages 62-64 of his booklet, **Belayev claimed:**
> The first passenger flight from Moscow to Lviv
> brought us to the newly liberated city. Not far

from the airport, two Messerschmitts (German fighter planes) appeared in the sky, and we were forced to sneak into the airport by flying just over the top of the High Castle. From the airport, which was in ruins, we had to walk to the center of Lviv...The Oblast Headquarters of the Communist Party was located in a small building at the end of Rbatska Street. Parked in the street were several military vehicles. When I asked the guard how to get to the Party Secretary, he pointed to a thin, dark-complexioned man in a Red Army general's uniform descending the stairs and said, 'There he is!'

When he approached, I introduced myself, and presented my orders. 'A writer? Very good!' he said, as he resumed walking. 'I would speak with you now, but I can't. A group of Ukrainian bandits has appeared in the town of Peremyshlyany, and I have to go there. Sign in, and find the representative of the Extraordinary Commission. They need a professional writer to help them prepare the materials concerning the Nazis' war crimes. Tell them that I sent you. Later, you and I will talk.'

Apparently, Belayev was no less of a "big-cheese" in the Soviet NKVD than Major Galski-Klym Dmytruk. Working with the Extraordinary Commission, Belayev wrote, he became very knowledgeable about the facts, the testimony of the witnesses, and the contents of various relevant documents. But, apparently, nowhere did he come upon any reference to the Nachtigall Battalion, its commanders, officers, or members. Only some forty years later, did Belayev suddenly "recall" the Battalion's supposed crimes in 1941.

Belayev claimed that he had worked closely with Dr. Zygmunt

Albert and had read the testimony of Mrs. Bartel, professor Bartel's wife. As the reader may recall, she had testified that her husband had been arrested on July 2, 1941, by three members of the Gestapo. She further testified that she took food parcels to her husband every day until July 26, on which day her parcel was refused. She was told that her husband had been executed earlier that morning on orders of Heinrich Himmler. By July 26, however, the Nachtigall Battalion had been gone from Lviv for three weeks and was stationed in the city of Vinnytsia! That fact also did not discourage Belayev, who confidently continued his fictional account:

> The Ukrainian nationalists in the Nachtigall Battalion, not finding Professor Bartel at home, brought some members of the SS to the Polytechnical Institute with them. There, an older SS officer met with Bartel in the professor's office…Suddenly, the doors flew open and Bandera's men saw the SS officer pushing Bartel out of the door, beating him over the head with the butt of his pistol. In a few hours, after a short interrogation in the Gestapo's torture chamber, Kasimierz Bartel, already half-dead, was thrown into the building's cellar and shot.

Later, Belayev threw in another inventive allegation: "It was Erich Koch who came up with a brilliant, devilish idea: to employ his loyal Ukrainian fascist slaves, the Ukrainian nationalists in the Nachtigall Battalion, to murder the Polish professors." Belayev must have read the testimonies of Olena Kukhar, Lanskoronska, the SS officers, and the testimony of Gestapo chief Krieger - all of whom testified that the arrests and murders of the Polish professors in Lviv had been the work of the Germans. Four decades later, that still did not deter Belayev from putting the blame on the Nachtigall Battalion.

Yet another confirmation of Belayev's complete lack of credibility was his explanation of the assassination of Ukrainian nationalist leader, Stepan Bandera, in 1959. On pages 94-95 of his book **Belayev** wrote:

> Suddenly, thunder from the heavens! On October 15, 1959, the teletype machines in newspaper editorial rooms around the globe reported that the bloodthirsty leader of the Ukrainian nationalists, Stepan Bandera, who was carrying a passport with the name Stepan Popel, was in critical condition in Munich, West Germany. Apparently he had fallen or been pushed from a third floor balcony of an apartment building. He was taken to the hospital, where he was pronounced dead. The homicide department of the West German Federal Criminal Police began its investigation...The investigators took their time, notwithstanding the fact that the papers were calling Bandera's death the 'Number One sensation.'

A few days later, however, a new version of Bandera's death began to circulate: an autopsy had discovered evidence of potassium cyanide in his body. People close to the investigation shrugged their shoulders. Why had it taken several days to discover the potassium cyanide in Bandera's body? Wouldn't poisoning by potassium cyanide have been evident immediately? The infamous Voice of America, trying to hide the killers' tracks, suggested that Bandera had committed suicide.

But Bandera's followers loudly protested: there was no way he would have killed himself. The East German newspaper, *Neue Deutschland (New Germany,* reported that Bandera, as one of the organizers of the massacres in Lviv in July 1941, was one of the witnesses to Theodor Oberlander's (his chief's) crimes there. The German paper emphasized the fact that since the end of the war, Oberlander had attempted to distance himself as much as possible from his former underling, the fascist Bandera. The Polish communist newspaper, *Trybuna Ludu* (*Tribune of the People*), commented that Oberlander's efforts to disassociate himself from Bandera had alarmed the latter, who lately had become concerned for his life.

In its October 19, 1959 issue, even the bourgeois paper *Suddeutsche Zeitung (BBC Newspaper)* opined that Bandera had been murdered…According to statements of his friends and associates, as an accomplice in Oberlander's criminal activities in Lviv, Bandera had recently begun to fear for his life…Bandera was poisoned by the followers of some very influential individuals…Bandera knew more about the Federal Minister in Bonn than Oberlander wanted him to know.

This same line was repeated by the East German newspaper, *Berliner Zeitung (Berlin Newspaper)* which declared that, "Bandera was silenced by a murder syndicate headed by General Gehlen, on orders from Oberlander." The head of the Munich police homicide bureau, a certain Schmidt, categorically declared, "It will be very difficult to find those responsible for the killing. It is most likely that we must look for them in circles to which the criminal police normally have no access."

Like his fellow Soviet propagandists, Belayev was not bothered by the facts and simply lied about Bandera's murder. The facts concerning Bandera's assassination had already been definitively established by a court in Karlsruhe, West Germany. We can all agree that Stepan Bandera was murdered by a "criminal syndicate", but that syndicate was headquartered in Moscow, and its name was the KGB. Bandera's assassination was not the first such murder committed by the Soviets against expatriate opponents of their regime. Symon Petlura, leader of the short-lived independent Ukrainian National Republic, was murdered in Paris in 1926. Yevhen Konovalets, the founder and leader of the OUN, was murdered in Rotterdam, Holland in 1938. Lev Rebet, a prominent Ukrainian journalist and leading member of a rival faction of the OUN, was murdered in 1957. Non-Ukrainian opponents of the Soviet and other communist regimes also have been assassinated in the West. The homicide investigator Schmidt was clearly correct in predicting that it would be difficult to find those responsible for Bandera's murder, because they were in Moscow and obviously not available for questioning by the West German police.

The short passages above should be sufficient to give the reader a good idea of the nature and quality of various Soviet publications which have attempted to discredit the Ukrainian independence movement. Unfortunately, similar publications continue to circulate today, more than twenty years after the collapse of the Soviet Union. Most of them, assuredly, emanate from the Kremlin in post-Soviet Russia.

Allegations Against the Nachtigall Battalion in Communist Poland

The communist press in Poland, like its "sister publications," first began making allegations against the Nachtigall Battalion in 1959, at the same time as the East Germans were beginning their campaign against Theodor Oberlander and the Nachtigall Battalion. The communist Polish press had previously written quite extensively about the Ukrainian Insurgent Army, but rarely had it mentioned the Nachtigall Battalion, and it never leveled any allegations of criminal wrongdoing against it. Only after the commencement of the court case in East Germany, did the press in the Soviet Union and Communist Poland begin attacking the Nachtigall Battalion.

Polish authors A. Szczesniak and B. Szota devoted considerable attention to the Nachtigall Battalion in their "documentary" volume entitled *Droga do Nikond* (*The Road to Nowhere*). It was supposedly written on the basis of archival materials concerning the Ukrainian Insurgent Army and its military activities in Eastern Galicia, along the so-called Curzon Line. The chapter beginning on page 108 of *Droga*...claimed that "...from the moment they entered Lwow and secured the radio station, the members of the Nachtigall Battalion, together with their commander Roman Shukhevych, began their terrorist activities. In fact, the major crimes which were committed in Lwow during that time were committed by the Nachtigall Battalion."

Szczesniak and Szota went on to write about the arrests of the Polish professors in Lviv. Repeating the claims of the Soviets and the East Germans, they added a few more names of victims and concluded, "In total, the Nachtigall Battalion murdered fifty-one professors and/or members of their families. Some of their victims were subjected to torture before being shot."

The authors were certainly familiar with the report of the Soviet Extraordinary Commission. One must assume that they had also read Dr. Zygmunt Albert's article in *Przeglond Lekarski (Medical Review),* which has been discussed earlier, as well as other articles which had appeared in the communist Polish press earlier. Notwithstanding the fact that the Extraordinary Commission, Zygmunt Albert's article and other articles which had previously appeared in the Polish press media all had placed the blame for the murders of the Polish professors entirely on the German SS, the authors of *Droga do Nikond* decided to place the blame on the Nachtigall Battalion. The authors were simply following the "new party line," which the Soviets and the East Germans adopted in 1959, with their attack on Oberlander, the West German

Government of Konrad Adenauer, and the Ukrainian independence movement.

A little later in their book, authors Szczesniak and Szota leveled an entirely new allegation against the Nachtigall Battalion: "At the same time, the fascists of the Nachtigall Battalion arrested and murdered almost one hundred Polish students. All together, the fascists of the Nachtigall Battalion and their Hitlerite allies murdered three thousand members of the Polish intelligentsia of Lwow." This was a completely new allegation, unsupported by any testimony or documentation, and can be dismissed summarily. The authors went on to allege that after leaving Lviv, the Nachtigall Battalion continued its murderous campaign in every town through which it passed: Zolochiv, Sataniv, Proskuriv and Vinnytsia. A reader completely unfamiliar with the historical facts might conclude that the Nachtigall Battalion was organized for the sole purpose of committing war crimes against Poles and murdering innocent civilians!

In 1960, Aleksander Drozdinski and Jan Zaborowski published a book entitled *Oberlander*, soon after the appearance of an East German book by the name of *Ein Braun Buch uber Oberlander* (*A Brown Book about Oberlander*), which had been mentioned previously. The authors of both books claimed that the Polish professors in Lviv had been arrested by the Wehrmacht, not the Gestapo, assisted by Oberlander and the Nachtigall Battalion. The authors added the charge that the lists of Polish professors to be arrested had been prepared for the Germans in Krakow by followers of Bandera.

Some twenty years after Stepan Bandera had been assassinated by a Soviet agent in Munich, and the "Oberlander Affair" of 1959-60 had long been forgotten, the communist press in Poland commemorated the 40th anniversary of the tragic events of July 1941 in Lviv, encouraging comments from its readers.

Among those commenting was Professor Zygmunt Albert, who

reminded the readers that he had written extensively about the events in Lviv, in *Przeglond Lekarski* and in his book *Lwowski Vidzal Lekarski w Czasie Okupaciji Hitlerowskej, 1941-1944* (*The Lwow Chapter of Doctors during the Hitlerite Occupation of 1941-1944*). Professor Albert refuted the allegations made by authors Drozdinski and Zaborowski and reaffirmed his previous conclusion that neither Theodor Oberlander nor the Nachtigall Battalion had participated in the murders of the Polish professors in Lviv in 1941. He emphasized, again, that the murders had been committed by special German units which had been formed for the specific purpose of murdering the Soviet and Polish intelligentsia, as well as the Jews of Lviv. Professor Albert repeated his comments during the solemn commemoration of the fortieth anniversary of the tragic events in Lviv in 1941, held at the Polish Academy of Sciences in Warsaw.

Edward Prus, Alexander Korman, and Victor Polishchuk

Mr. Prus, another communist propagandist, is often cited as an authority on the Nachtigall Battalion and its supposed activities in Lviv in July 1941. During its seventy years in power, the Soviet government never lost its fear and hatred of "nationalism". The Soviets invariably and maliciously slandered the nationalistic/patriotic sentiments of the countries which they held captive, attempting often to manipulate the nationalistic sentiments of one against another. After the Second World War, the Soviets attempted mightily to redirect the hatred of the Poles away from Soviet Russia and toward Ukrainian nationalists. To achieve this goal, the Kremlin recruited a number of historians, including F. Friedman in Lviv, H. Wasser and R. Auerbach in Warsaw, S. Krakowski in Lodz, and M. Gergarda, J. Wilczur, Alexander Korman, Edward Prus, and Viktor Polishchuk (Wiktor Poliszczuk). Their assignment was to conduct "historical research" and publish scurrilous books and pamphlets whose express purpose was to discredit Ukrainian "nationalists" and the Ukrainian independence movement as a whole. Naturally, the recruited "scholars" were expected to produce histories in keeping with the ideological and political requirements specified by their Soviet and/or local communist employers.

In a relatively short time, the various "scholars" finished their assignments and produced an impressive body of pseudo-historical, but transparently propagandistic literature. With help from the government-controlled educational establishment and state-run media, this "historical literature" acquired a certain authoritativeness. Younger, largely ill-informed historians, often naively and uncritically accepted the writings of Prus, et al., to be accurate and truthful accounts of historical events. Of course, this is exactly what the Soviets had intended. Soviet Communists have conducted a long-lasting and generally successful campaign of disinformation and lies, using their in-house and contract "historians." As a result, opinion polls have suggested that as recently as the 1990s, Ukraine was the nation most disliked by the the Poles. This animosity had no rational basis. Ukrainian armies or police forces had never occupied Polish ethnic lands and had never politically, culturally, or economically dominated or oppressed the Poles. This Polish animosity toward Ukrainians was, undoubtedly, intentionally fostered and encouraged by the malicious writings of Prus and his companions. Among other things, Prus had alleged that Ukrainian nationalists had "sewn rats into the intestines" of captive Poles. The rats would supposedly eat their way through the victims' organs and exit their bodies through the heart. Soviet-inspired propaganda even blamed Ukrainians for putting down the Warsaw Uprising and conducting mass killings of Poles near Czestochowa.

Prus and others in his group of "historians" also claimed that Ukrainian nationalists had murdered 500,000 Poles in Volhynia in the 1940s. The absurdity of this claim becomes patently obvious when one considers the official census figures from 1940, which put the number of Poles living in Volhynia at roughly 300,000.

Furthermore, almost half of Volhynia's Polish residents were forcibly uprooted and exiled by the Soviets in 1939-40, when they "liberated" Volhynia in the aftermath of the infamous Molotov-Ribbentrop Pact with Nazi Germany. That would have left a population of approximately 150,000 Poles in Volhynia.

Now, let's look briefly at Victor Polishchuk. He is the author of a 500-page anti-Ukrainian diatribe published in Toronto, Canada, entitled *Hirka Pravda* (*The Bitter Truth*). The book fiercely attacks the Ukrainian independence movement during the Second World War. An entire chapter is devoted to the Nachtigall and Roland Battalions. In his introduction Polishchuk claims to be an ethnic Ukrainian from Volhynia, who lived in Poland from 1946 through 1981 before immigrating to Canada. In Poland, he had been a teacher, a lawyer, and a government prosecutor. The fact that Polishchuk had been a prosecutor in communist Poland and a member of the communist apparatus is reason enough to doubt his credibility and his allegations concerning the Nachtigall Battalion. Polishchuk's ideological mindset and motives with respect to Ukrainian nationalism and the Ukrainian independence movement only increase the reader's level of suspicion concerning his credibility. The book was published in Poland and in Ukraine. Pyotr Symonenko, leader of the Communist Party and a member of Ukraine's Verkhovna Rada (Parliament), soon began referring to Polishchuk as an "authority" on the Organization of Ukrainian Nationalists and the Ukrainian Insurgent Army.

What was the attitude of fair-minded Poles towards Polishchuk? In a letter to the Congress of Canadian Polonia, dated June 9, 1994, the **Polish Historical Society in the United States** stated the following:

> …One of the loyal servants of the Soviet Empire was the former communist lawyer Viktor Polishchuk…from Volhynia or Lwow (Lviv), who had changed his name during or just after the Second World War… We have received

information from Poland that several years ago, while Poland was still governed by the communist regime, the State Security Service sent Polishchuk to Canada for the purpose of inflaming animosity and hatred between Ukrainians and Poles there. Similar assignments had been given earlier to Lviv residents S. Gerhard, Edward Prus, and J. Wilczur. In the United States, M. Hanusyak, an ethnic Ukrainian, had been the KGB's agent for many years. We are unsure as to whether A. Korman was also a Soviet agent.

...In July 1994, Viktor Polishchuk was soliciting funds in the Polish-American community to help him publish his book, *Hirka Pravda (Bitter Truth)* in Polish. We asked him for a copy of his book in Ukrainian, so that we could review it. Not only did he refuse to provide us with a copy, but he also declined our request for copies of any reviews which may have appeared concerning his book.

We suspect that the majority of the sources which Polishchuk cites were from the files of the KGB, in which every one of the supposed 'witnesses' was exaggerating his or her testimony concerning alleged war crimes, perhaps with the hope of obtaining greater compensation from the German or Polish governments. The former head of the Polish Communist Security Service, Professor Pilichowicz, had a special file which he labeled *Bzdury (Nonsense)*. After Pilichowicz's death, the communist Polish Security Service continued to use the *Bzdury* files in their ongoing war against the West German government of Konrad Adenauer, and in their efforts to destroy the Polish and Ukrainian independence movements...

Let's consider some of Polishchuk's claims, for which he relied heavily on the similarly "authoritative" writings of his communist-era colleague, Edward Prus, and upon a booklet written by Oleksander Korman, entitled *Z Kryvavykh Dniv u Lvovi, 1941.* (*From the Bloody Days in Lviv, 1941*). On page 176 of his book **Polishchuk** wrote:

> Oleksander Korman's booklet, published in London in 1990, describes the tragedy of the Jews and Poles in Lviv, and particularly of the Polish academics.
>
> They died martyrs' deaths at the hands of the Hitlerites, soldiers of the Nachtigall Battalion, and civilian nationalists during the days between July 1-3, 1941....Korman not only describes the bloody Bacchanalia, but relates the testimony of witnesses and lists his sources.

Polishchuk continued:

> Ukrainian nationalist historians and publicists deny the involvement of the Organization of Ukrainian Nationalists in the murders of the Polish professors and Jews in Lviv. But here, in Korman's materials, are vivid descriptions of the facts, the names of witnesses, and other information confirming the author's objectivity.

Polishchuk attacked the Nachtigall Battalion and leveled various charges against it on page 178 of his book:

> The members of the Nachtigall Battalion led communists and Poles out of their homes and simply hanged them on lamp posts, telephone poles or from balconies. As an individual who had been arrested walked out of the corridor, he would receive a heavy blow on the top of his skull from

142

behind and fall. A Ukrainian standing over him, armed with a bayonet, would jab the bayonet into the victim's abdomen or heart. Other Ukrainians would drag the bodies to the side and throw them onto a wagon. The residents of Lviv called the men of the Nachtigall Battalion "little birds" because of the insignia on their automobiles and motorcycles. The "little birds" were also on their German uniforms, which bore German military insignia. They spoke in Ukrainian, and had blue and yellow ribbons tied to their bayonets and never associated with Poles, except when they took part in the beatings or executions. On Ruska and Boyim Streets they shot a number of Polish students, who had been dragged there by a group of Ukrainian nationalists. We were taken to the prison on Lontzki street. There were 500 of us Jews, and almost all of us were killed by Ukrainians...

This material was lifted entirely from Korman's booklet, but was somewhat "embellished" by Polishchuk. Now, let's compare some of Polishchuk's claims with the writings of Korman. On page 8 of his book, **Korman wrote**:

...The Ukrainian soldiers were already in Lviv on Monday, April 24, 1941. That day after lunch, the Ukrainians began dragging Jews out of their apartments and taking them to the square in front of the Velykyj Theatre. There were several thousand people there, men and women. They were ordered to clean the square, but weren't provided anything with which to do so. Ukrainian soldiers stood around and beat them. The Jews were required to walk through a *shpalir* (gamut) while Ukrainians beat them mercilessly. Many of the Jews died on the spot, and others were seriously injured..."

143

Can an objective reader believe such nonsense? That Ukrainian soldiers from the Nachtigall Battalion had occupied Lviv in April of 1941, two months before the German attack on the Soviet Union, dragged Jews out of their homes and beat them to death? In April 1941, Lviv was still under Soviet occupation, and the NKVD was brutalizing and murdering its victims.

On page 10, Korman continues: "The Germans looked on impassively as Ukrainian nationalists, drenched in sweat and breathing heavily, dragged bloodied Jews out of their homes and conducted blood baths in the city's plazas." Korman offers his own, skewed interpretation of the events: "The world had not seen, and history had not recorded, something this terrible since the time of Genghis Khan. The world was turned upside down, the circle of history was turned back to the very beginning..."

Continuing with **Korman's account**, on page 13, we read the purported testimony of a surviving victim of the Nachtigall Battalion, supposedly an engineer at the Lviv Polytechnical Institute at the time:

> During the time of the executions on the Kurtymiv Hills, one of the victims who had been shot earlier, was able to run away...He was a chemical engineer by profession who worked at the Polytechnical Institute before the war. He was arrested on July 1, and taken to the prison on Pelczynska Street...That same evening, he was taken to the old Brygidka prison, together with other prisoners. All of them were led into a corridor and held in such tight confines that they had to relieve themselves where they stood.
>
> After a period of time, the names of prisoners were called out, and one-by-one they were directed to the doors leading into the prison courtyard. As they were walking out, they were struck on the head with

hammers from behind the door... The victim would fall, and a Ukrainian standing over him, armed with a rifle tipped with a bayonet, would impale the victim in the abdomen or heart. At the very moment that the engineer was about to receive a blow to the head, a German officer dressed in a uniform of the Wehrmacht appeared and ordered that the killing be stopped. He instructed the soldiers to stand back...

Korman was supposedly relating the testimony of a witness who could be identified. We are told that he was a chemical engineer and worked at the Polytechnical Institute in Lviv. Presumably, his name could be determined from the school's records and his identity ascertained. But, Korman never identified him! The same occurred with the other purported surviving witnesses.

There were many other such supposed "testimonies" of unnamed, unidentified eyewitnesses related by Korman, which were repeated almost *verbatim* by Polishchuk. Not in a single instance, in either publication, was the name of a witness given, so that he or she could be questioned. In reality, of course, both authors had a single purpose in mind and the truth did not matter. In fact, the greater the lie, the more outrageous the allegation, the more horrendous the crime which could be blamed on the Ukrainian nationalists, the greater would be the reward for Korman, Polishchuk and the others, and their future career in the Communist propaganda machine would be secure.

As a member of the Nachtigall Battalion which together with the Roland Battalion was later reorganized as the Shutzmannshaftsbattalion-201, I state unequivocally that the members of the Battalions never wore black German uniforms or German military or other insignia as claimed by Korman and Company. Nor did we ever carry bayonets "adorned" with blue and yellow ribbons. I also unequivocally affirm that at no time during the period of our involvement and cooperation with the

German Wehrmacht in western Ukraine as members of the Nachtigall Battalion, or in Belarus as members of Shutzmannshaftsbattalion-201, did we receive any orders from our commanding officers to commit any act or acts of violence against the civilian population in the occupied territories, nor were we implicitly led by anyone to believe that we should do so. Furthermore, I never witnessed any member of the Nachtigall Battalion or the Shutzmannshaftsbattalion-201 commit any act of abuse or violence against any civilian, of any nationality or religion, Polish, Jewish, or otherwise, contrary to the many fanciful and horrific allegations which have appeared in the works of Korman, Polishchuk and others. I never saw a single civilian victim lying in the street or hanging from a lamp post or balcony while my comrades in the Nachtigall Battalion and I were in Lviv between June 30 and July 5, 1941. Furthermore, I never heard any member of the Battalion "brag" about committing any such act and never heard any rumors of such conduct by any member of the Nachtigall Battalion.

Other Examples of Soviet Disinformation

Another example of the Soviet use of disinformation and falsehood related to the "Oberlander Affair" was the Soviet spin on the death of Stepan Bandera, the leader of OUN-B. He was found dead in the stairwell of his apartment in Munich, West Germany, on October 15, 1959, at the very height of the anti-Oberlander, anti-Nachtigall campaign. At Bandera's funeral, the officiating priest declared that Bandera must have died at the hands of a Soviet assassin. The Soviet and East German press quickly responded to the clergyman's assertion (which later proved to be absolutely true) and suggested that Bandera had been ordered killed by none other than Theodor Oberlander. *Krasnaya Zvyezda* (*Red Star*), the official publication of the Soviet Ministry of Defense, opined that Oberlander had Bandera killed to prevent him from testifying against Oberlander in the East German court proceedings. The paper claimed that Bandera had entered Lviv on June 30, 1941, with the Nachtigall Battalion and simply "knew too much" about Oberlander's role in the crimes which the Battalion committed there. *Komsomolskaya Pravda* (*Komsomol Truth*), the official paper of the Communist Youth League, faithfully repeated *Krasnaya Zvyezda's* accusations against Oberlander. It even printed a cartoon showing Oberlander standing over Bandera's coffin, saying, "He was a good Nazi. Unfortunately, he knew too much about me."

Other Soviet newspapers also blamed Oberlander for Bandera's death. The East German ADN *(Allgemeiner Deutscher Nachrichtendienst)* a German General News Service, however, was circulating a different version of Bandera's demise. It claimed that Bandera had been shot by one Myskiw, a Ukrainian émigré, on orders of the West German intelligence service. Later, the inventive East Germans claimed that Myskiw was also murdered by the West Germans, supposedly to silence him about the West German government's role in Bandera's murder.

The criminal investigation of the West German prosecutor into the allegations made against Oberlander by the Communist-Front organization determined that "Myskiw" had been in Italy on the day of Bandera's death and could not have killed Bandera. It also found that Myskiw died in 1960 of natural causes. The prosecutor's report included reports from the West German intelligence agency. The West Germans had intercepted coded Soviet cables instructing their agents in the West to disseminate the "Myskiw version" of Bandera's murder. Subsequent intercepted cables from Moscow to its agents in the West inquired whether the "Myskiw version" had been effective and was still worth spreading. The Summary in the West German prosecutor's report included the following conclusion concerning the Soviets' efforts to cover up their role in ordering Bandera's assassination: "The propaganda initiated in the East German zone, pursuant to the orders of the Soviets, was intended to blame the West German government for the death of Bandera. It was typical of Communist propaganda to blame someone else, preferably someone in a foreign country, for its own misdeeds."

There was yet another example of Soviet efforts to plant disinformation in the Oberlander affair. This one involved falsehoods concerning Dr. A. Hertzner, the German officer who commanded the Nachtigall Battalion in 1941. A "breaking news report" appeared in East Germany announcing the "recent death, under suspicious circumstances" of Dr. Hertzner. The report noted that Hertzner had been the commander of the Nachtigall Battalion during the Second World War and suggested that Theodor Oberlander was responsible for his death. Oberlander's motive, claimed the news report, was to prevent Hertzner from testifying against him! The authors of the spurious East German report did not know (or did not care) that Hertzner had died in 1942 of wounds he had suffered in battle, and he was buried in the Cemetery of Heroes in Potsdam. This information was provided to Berlin radio station PIAC on November 2, 1959, by his widow, Ketti Hertzner, after she happened to read the East German report of her husband's "recent" death. She also notified the prosecutor who was conducting the investigation.

In 1962, it was clearly established that the actual murderer of Stepan Bandera was Bohdan Stashynsky, an agent of the Soviet KGB and, ironically, a Ukrainian. Stashynsky was given the highest order of commendation from his superiors in the KGB for the successful completion of his "special assignments:" the assassination of two prominent Ukrainian nationalist leaders living in the West - Stepan Bandera, in 1959, and before him, Lev Rebet, in 1957. On October 12, 1961, Stashynsky defected while visiting West Berlin. He surrendered to the Americans, who turned him over to the West German authorities for prosecution after debriefing him. Bohdan Stashynsky was tried for the murders of Rebet and Bandera in a West German court. He confessed, was found guilty, and was sentenced to an eight-year prison term. After spending seven years in a West German prison, Stashynsky was released and given a new identity by the American intelligence community. As the West German court noted in its decision, however, the Soviet Government was the party primarily responsible for the murders of the two Ukrainian émigré leaders. It was the Soviet KGB which trained Stashynsky, ordered him to assassinate Lev Rebet and Stepan Bandera, provided him with the necessary weapons, and later rewarded him for the "successful completion" of his assignments.

The West German prosecutor's investigation determined conclusively that Stepan Bandera could not have been with the Nachtigall Battalion when it entered Lviv on June 30, 1941, since he was in German custody in Berlin. The prosecutor concluded that the assassination of Bandera had no relation to the proceedings concerning Theodor Oberlander, but was carried out on the orders of the Soviet Government. The prosecutor's investigation and findings illustrated, once again, the nefarious methods used by the Soviets in pursuing their policies and goals. In the Communist system the political authorities and the courts were inseparable in their total disregard for the truth.

Summary and Conclusions

As the reader already knows, the Nachtigall and Roland Battalions were disbanded by the Germans in mid-July 1941, and later combined and reorganized into Shutzmanshafstbattalion-201. The members of the Schutzmannshaftsbattalion-201 were discharged at the end of December 1942, after refusing to renew their contracts to serve with the Germans. The officers and men were fortunate to avoid the execution squad.

The majority of the men in the three battalions soon joined the Ukrainian underground and became partisan-soldiers in the Ukrainian Insurgent Army (Ukrayinska Povstanska Armiya - UPA). There they became officers and instructors under the command of Roman Shukhevych, the former political commander of the Nachtigall Battalion. His name, especially his *nom de guerre,* "Taras Chuprynka", would become widely known and greatly respected among Ukrainians. Some of the former members of the Nachtigall, Roland and Schuzmannshaftsbattlion-201 battalions joined other Ukrainian military formations. One of these was the Waffen-SS Galicia Division, which fought against the Soviets on the Eastern Front and against Communist partisans in Slovakia and the Balkans from 1943 to 1945.

Nazi Germany was at the zenith of its power and influence at the beginning of the 1940s. Hitler was intoxicated by his early triumphs and was confident that no other country could successfully challenge his German armies. He also believed, unrealistically, that Germany would be able to conquer and govern the Soviet Union on its own, without the support of non-Germans. For this reason, he refused to deal with representatives of the nations which were or had been under Soviet occupation. However, there were ongoing contacts between representatives of the captive nations and certain circles in the German army. These groups, unlike the top Nazi leadership, understood that Germany could not defeat the Soviets and maintain effective control over the vast territories of Eastern Europe without recognizing the captive people's rights to freedom and some form of independent statehood. Unfortunately, it was not the German army but Hitler and his inner circle who made the political decisions.

Knowing the ultimate goal of the OUN-B led by Stepan Bandera, the political leadership of Nazi Germany used every method at its disposal to frustrate the Organization's efforts. Bandera was arrested by the Gestapo and held in Berlin to prevent him from entering Lviv and directly influencing events in Ukraine. The Ukrainian National Committee in Krakow was also disbanded.

Why didn't the Germans break up the National Meeting in Lviv on June 30, 1941, at which the participants proclaimed the renewal of Ukrainian statehood and independence? Why didn't the Germans arrest Yaroslav Stetsko and other OUN-B leaders on the spot or beforehand, to prevent them from proclaiming Ukrainian independence? I believe that they did not do so because of the presence of the Nachtigall Battalion in Lviv. The members of the Battalion had sworn allegiance to the OUN, to a free Ukraine, and to the interim Ukrainian government. The Nachtigall Battalion had occupied important strategic objectives in the city, including the radio station, the electric power station, the natural gas plant, and the citadel. The Germans realized that there would be a confrontation with the Ukrainians if they forcibly disbanded the June 30 meeting, and that such a confrontation would interfere with their advance into central and eastern Ukraine.

For several momentous days, the Ukrainian radio station, symbolically named in honor of Yevhen Konovalets (founder and first leader of the Organization of Ukrainian Nationalists from 1929 until his assasination in 1938), was Ukrainian Galicia's lifeline to the world. The station remained in Ukrainian hands for three days, until the Gestapo took it over by force. During those three momentous days the world was able to learn of the aspirations of Ukrainians for statehood and their bold declaration of independence.

The June 30, 1941, proclamation of Ukrainian statehood and independence, widely broadcast over the radio, reverberated throughout Galicia and beyond. Ukrainian citizens began organizing massive celebrations and demonstrations, holding civic meetings, and organizing local government administrations. Thousands of members of the so-called Pokhidni Hrupy (Advance Groups) consisted mainly of OUN members from western Ukraine, Poland, Germany, Austria, and Czechoslovakia. They moved eastward to help organize Ukrainian community life in the territories recently abandoned by the Soviets. They carried news of freedom to the millions of Ukrainians in central and eastern Ukraine, who had been forced to endure life under Communist tyranny.

The proclamation of Ukrainian statehood was an historical and politically symbolic act. It surprised, displeased, and disturbed the leadership of Nazi Germany, which in its Aryan arrogance could not envision or accept an independent Ukraine. The Germans hesitated to arrest the leaders of the interim Ukrainian government or declare its proclamation of independence "null and void" while the Nachtigall Battalion remained in Lviv and in Galicia. It was only when the Nachtigall Battalion was far from Lviv, near Vinnytisa in the Podolya region, did the Gestapo begin arresting members of the Ukrainian government.

In order to isolate eastern Galicia from the rest of Ukraine, the Germans attached it to the General Governement, which included Poland and parts of Belarus. The central and eastern Ukrainian lands were made part of the Reichskommisariat Ukraine. Ukrainians of eastern Galicia were attached to an administrative territory, the majority of whose inhabitants were Poles openly hostile to the political aspirations of Ukrainians. The Germans soon began liquidating members of the Advance Groups which had reached central and eastern Ukraine, many of whom they shot at Babyn Yar in Kyiv. They arrested the leadership and prominent members of the OUN in Galicia and executed or interned them in concentration camps.

On July 11, 1941, the Germans arrested Premier Yaroslav Stetsko and other members of the Interim Ukrainian Government. They took them to Germany, where they were interned for the remainder of the war. Upon learning of these arrests, members of both the Nachtigall and the Roland Battalions protested the German action and categorically refused further cooperation with the Wehrmacht. By doing so, the members of both Ukrainian Battalions knowingly subjected themselves to serious reprisals by the Germans.

I am firmly convinced that had the Nachtigall Battalion not been in Lviv on June 30, 1941, the Germans would have prevented the public proclamation of Ukrainian statehood and independence by arresting Yaroslav Stetsko and the entire Ukrainian leadership. Had the city's radio station not been in the hands of the Nachtigall Battalion, the world would not have learned of Ukraine's declaration of independence, and the OUN's Advance Groups would not have been able to move as deeply into central and eastern Ukraine as they did.

Had there been no Nachtigall, Roland or Schutzmannshaftsballion-*201* Battalions, there would have been no pool of experienced, battle-tested instructors to train officers for the Ukrainian Insurgent Army, officers who led the thousands of volunteers in the UPA who heroically fought against the Germans and Soviets. For this reason, no amount of calumny which some may heap on the Organization of Ukrainian Nationalists (OUN), the Legion of Ukrainian Nationalists (DUN), the Nachtigall, Roland and Schutzmannshaftsbattalion-201 Battalions, the Ukrainian Insurgent Army, or the Galicia Division can dishonor them in the eyes of informed, patriotic Ukrainians, and all people, who cherish liberty and freedom.

I am grateful to the Creator that the blood spilled by my comrades in the ranks of the Nachtigall Battalion, its successor the Schutzmanshaftsbattalion-201, and in other Ukrainian patriotic, military, and political formations was not spilled in vain. I am thankful and proud that their heroic deeds, for which millions of their courageous compatriots sacrificed their lives and set an honorable example for the current generation of Ukrainians, who live in an independent Ukraine.

I am proud of my service in the Nachtigall Battalion, in Schutzmannschaftsbattalion-201, and in the Ukrainian Insurgent Army (UPA). I am gratified to have had the opportunity to contribute to the cause of Ukrainian freedom and independence.

Myroslaw Kalba
2012

PART THREE

Photographs

Roman Shukhevych, political commander of the Battalion Nachtigall

Members of the future Nachtigall Battalion in Krynytsya, in the Carpathian Mountains, wearing the uniform of the Arbeitsdinst, prior to being sent to Neuhammer, Silesia for basic training. Standing 3rd form right is the author, Myroslaw Kalba.

Members of the Nachtigall Battalion in Neuhammer, Silesia.

Roman Shukhevych, Supreme Commander of the Ukrainian Insurgent Army (UPA). Many soldiers of the Nachtigall Battalion later joined the UPA.

Myroslaw Kalba, with his cousin Myroslaw Bilynsky, in Krakow, Poland after returning from western Ukraine following the deactivation of the Nachtigall Battalion.

Fr. Ivan Hrynyokh, chaplain of the Nachtigall Battalion.

Officers of the Schuttsmanschaftsbattalion - 201 in Belarus. Standing in the center is Major Yevhen Pobihushchyj, the highest ranking Ukrainian officer and military commander of the Battalion.

Members of the Nachtigall Battalion with their chaplain after religious services in Krakow, Poland.

Company Commander Roman Kashubynsky, 4th from left, with his men in western Ukraine.

Schuttsmanschaftsbattalion – 201 in action in the forests of Belarus

Members of the Nachtigall Battalion in Belarus during religious services conducted by chaplain Vsevolod Durbak.

Ukrainian officers and non-commissioned officers of the Schuttsmanschaftsbattalion-201 in Belarus. Roman Shukhevych, political commander of the Battalion, is 2nd from the left in the front row.

Maps

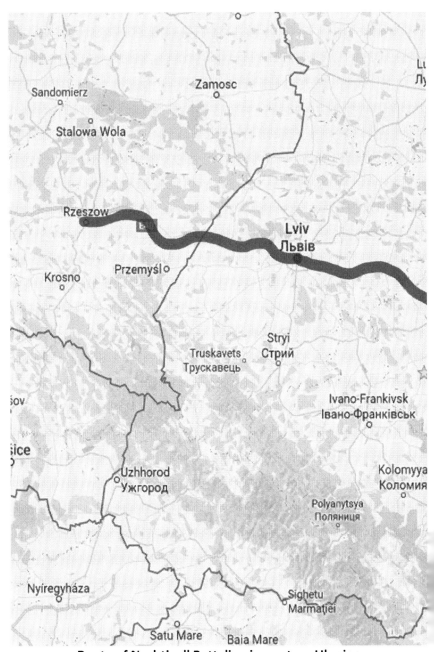
Route of Nachtigall Battalion in western Ukraine

Route of Nachtigall Battalion in western Ukraine

Epilogue

Is the history of the *Nachtigall* Battalion still relevant today? A 2015 television documentary produced by Hollywood director Oliver Stone clearly underscores this relevance.

Stone's documentary, entitled *The Untold History of the U.S.,* purports to present unknown historical facts. In Episode 4, titled *The Cold War: Truman, Wallace, Stalin, Churchill & the Bomb,* Stone portrays President Harry Truman as a "warmonger." His decision to use the atomic bomb in Japan provoked Stalin to occupy Eastern Europe, in order to defend the Soviet Union against probable American aggression. James Forrestal, then Secretary of Defense, is portrayed as a paranoid maniac. He, along with the CIA, was instrumental in organizing émigré Ukrainians into a military unit under the code-name *Nachtigall.* They were to be used for the purpose of parachuting diversionary forces into the Soviet Union. Mr. Stone went on to claim that the code-name *Nachtigall* was chosen by Forrestal to honor the *Nachtigall* Battalion of 1941, which allegedly murdered Poles and Jews!

Oliver Stone's revisionist history was, of course, not new at all, but simply a reiteration of the old Soviet propaganda. Such articles appeared regularly in the Soviet-controlled press, including the *Communist Daily News,* which was published in New York City during the Cold War.

Falsehoods, propaganda, and disinformation similar to Oliver Stone's documentary are regularly published and disseminated by the current authoritarian regime in Russia. The Kremlin's propaganda machine justifies Russia's illegal seizure of Crimea in 2014 and its support for terrorists in eastern Ukraine against the Ukrainian "fascist" regime. Russia's propagandists in the West follow the teachings of Nazi propaganda minister Goebbels very closely: the bigger the lie and the more often repeated – the more likely that gullible people will believe it.

The story of the Nachtigall Battalion is also instructive for the present. It is especially relevant to the tense political and military situation which exists in Europe today. Russia's armed seizure of Ukrainian territory in flagrant violation of international law is very similar to the policies of both Hitler and Stalin.

Ukrainian nationalists in the 1940s – unlike Ukraine's current political leaders, fully understood that Ukraine needed a strong and viable military if it was to gain and protect its independence. The men of the Nachtigall Battalion were willing to deal with the German army in order to obtain the training needed to form the officer corps for a future Ukrainian army. They knew that they had to rely on their own resources.

In contrast, Ukraine's leaders from 1991 through April 2014 recklessly and irresponsibly assumed that their country was safe from attack and had no need for an effective army. Had they really known and understood the history of Ukraine's long struggle for independence, including the history of the Nachtigall Battalion, they might have acted differently.

Glossary

Abwehr -
German military intelligence organization from 1921- 1944.

Anschluss -
occupation and annexation of Austria by Nazi Germany (1938).

Bacchanalia -
a drunken orgy.

Bandera, Stepan –
leader of the largest faction of the Organizatin of Ukrainian Nationalists (OUN-B) from 1940-1943 and from 1945-1959.

Banderites –
followers of Stepan Bandera.

Belarus –
country bordering Ukraine to the north.

Bereza Kartuska –
Polish political prisoner camp.

Blitzkrieg –
a swift and sudden attack, effectively utilized by the German Army during WWII.

Bundestag –
federal parliament of Germany.

CHEKA –
an acronym for "Chrezvychainaya kommisiya…All-Russian Extraordinary Committee to Combat Counter- Revolution and Sabotage," the secret police founded in 1917 by the Bolshevik government and reorganized in 1922 as the GPU; historical acronyms for other Russian secret intelligence units.
see also: **MVD, NKVD, OGPU, KGB**

Cossacks –
famous Ukrainian and Russian warriors and cavalrymen first reported in the 16th century.

Curatorial –
an administrative district.

173

Decalogue –
the "ten commandments" of the Organization of Ukrainian Nationalists (OUN).

DUN –
Druzhyny Ukrayinskykh Natsionalistiv (Legion of Ukrainian Nationalists) a military unit comprised of 660 men (mostly former OUN members) who volunteered to serve with the German Army in the war against the Soviets.

Einsatzgruppen –
special unit for liquidating Jews and perceived enemies of the Nazis.

Einsatzkommando –
commander in charge of the Einsatzgruppen.

Entente –
alliance between France, Great Britain, and Russia during WWI. It later included the U.S.

Frankfurt-an-der-Oder –
a city in the eastern part of Germany.

Gendarmerie –
military police.

Genghis Khan –
Mongol/Tatar conqueror in the 13th century.

German SD –
a member of the Nazi (Social Democratic) Party.

Gestapo –
the Nazi secret police.

Gulag –
Russian prison or forced labor camp for political prisoners.

Gymnasium –
high school.

Hapsburgs –
the ruling dynasty of the Austro-Hungarian Empire.

Hauptsturnfuhrer –
captain in the SS divisions.

Jewish Bund - .
Jewish League.

Judenrat –
Jewish organization created by the Nazis for the purpose of maintaining order and control of Jewish communities, and for confiscating valuables from the Jews.

KGB –
Komityet Gosudarstvennoi Bezopasnosti (Committee for State Security) the national security agency of the Soviet Union, 1954-1991.

Kremlin –
the citadel in Moscow housing the Soviet government.

Kulaks –
independent Ukrainian farmers; they were generally opposed to the Soviets' program of forced collectivization. A punishment, many were exiled to Siberia and other regions of Soviet Russia, while many others died during the famine of 1932- 1933.

Lemberg –
German name for the city of Lviv, Ukraine.

Lviv –
largest city in Western Ukraine.

Lvov –
Russian name for the city of Lviv.

Lwow –
Polish name for the city of Lviv.

MVD –
Ministerstvo Vnutrennikh Del (Ministry of Internal Affairs) the secret police of the Soviet Union, 1946-1991.

Magdeburg –
city in the eastern part of Germany.

Mein Kampf (*My Struggle*) -
Adolf Hitler's book which became the basis of the Nazi philosophy.

Melnyk, Andrii –
leader of the more moderate faction of the OUN.

Mogilev –
city in eastern Belarus, on the Dnipro River.

Molotov cocktails –
small, crude bombs made of bottles filled with flammable liquid.

Myrosio –
nickname for Myroslaw.

Myroslav –
a different transliteration of the name Myroslaw.

NKVD - *Narodnyy Komissariat Vnutrennikh Del*
(People's Commissariat for Internal Affairs) was the secret police organization of the Soviet Union which existed 1934 - 1954.

Nachtigall –
German for nightingale.

Neuhammer –
city in Silesia, a region between Czechoslovakia and Poland.

Nuremberg –
city in western Germany where the trials of Nazi war criminals took place.

Obengruppenfuhrer –
a high ranking Nazi military leader.

OGPU - *Obedinennoe Gossudarstvennoe Politicheskoe Upravleniye* (United State Political Administration) - the Soviet secret police from 1923 to 1934.

OUN - **Organization of Ukrainian Nationalists** (OUN)
is a disciplined, clandestine, revolutionary organization founded in 1929, whose goal was the creation of a free and independent Ukrainian State.

OUN-B –
the OUN faction led by Stepan Bandera.
Oblasts –
counties in Ukraine.
Peremyshl –
Ukrainian spelling of the city of Przemysl.
Petliura, Symon –
commander of the army of the Ukrainian Republic, 1918-1922.
Pilsudski, Marshall –
president of Poland, 1921-1929.
Presidium of the Central Committee –
Soviet executive branch
Prosvita –
Enlightenment Society.
Przemysl –
Polish spelling of the city of Peremyshl

Reichskommisariat –
administration of the Nazi government.
Reichsminister –
a member of the Nazi government.
Roland –
code name of one of the two battalions comprised of 660 Ukrainian volunteers, which participated in the invasion of Soviet Union on June 22, 1941.

SA –
Sturmabteilung attack units referred to as storm troopers or brown shirts, which were the paramilitary wing of the Nazi Party in the 1920s and 1930s. Originally, the SS was a section of the SA, but became fully autonomous in 1934.
SD - Sicherheitsdienst des Reichsführers-
SS, or SD, was the intelligence agency of the SS and the Nazi Party.
SS -
acronym for Schutzstaffel; a section of the Nazi militia used for maintaining order.

Schutzmannshaftsbattalion 201-
a police security unit subordinated to the _Wehrmacht._

Schutzstaffel –
small military guard unit.

St. George –
English version of the name St. Yurii.

St. Yurii Cathedral –
the Ukrainian Greek Catholic Cathedral in Lviv, Ukraine

Sheptytsky, Metropolitan Andrej –
hierarch of the Ukrainian Greek Catholic Church from the early 1900s until his death in 1944; a great patriot, he was the most influential figure among Ukrainians in Galicia.

Sonderkommando (SD) –
special unit assigned to round up, incarcerate, and execute Jews during Nazi Germany's occupation of Europe during WWII.

status quo ante –
previous condition.

Stetsko, Yaroslav –
premier of the short-lived Ukrainian State proclaimed by OUN B on June 30, 1941.

stukachi –
literally "those who knock." Prisoners used by Soviet prison authorities to spy and report on other prisoners in exchange for better treatment.

Sturmbanfuhrer –
rank of an officer in the SS units.

Ternopil –
third largest city in Galicia.

Trotsky, Leon –
revolutionary name of Leon Bronstein, one of the leaders of the Russian Bolshevik revolution; later banished from the Soviet Union by Josef Stalin, on whose orders he was murdered in 1940, in Mexico City.

Ukaz –
decree by the Russian tsar or other ruler.

Untersturmfuhrer –
   lower officer's rank in the SS units.
UPA - *Ukrayinska Povstanska Armiya* –
   (Ukrainian Insurgent Army). A partisan/guerilla force, which
   opposed both the Germans and Soviets during WWII. It
   continued the struggle for Ukrainian freedom and
   independence into the early 1950s. Its officer core was
   composed of many men who had been members of the
   Nachtigall Battalion.

Versailles Peace Treaty –
   the peace treaty drawn up by the winning Entente following
   World War I.
Volksdeutcher –
   an ethnic German born and living in another country.

Waffen –
   the official German term for the Ukrainian SS Galician
   Division.
Waffen SS Galizien Division –
   a division of Ukrainian volunteers created by the German
   government, with the approval of the Ukrainian Central
   Committee to fight the Soviets on the Eastern Front, in the
   waning years of WWII.
Wehrmacht –
   German Army during WWII.
Weimar Republic –
   the name for Germany from 1919 to 1933.

Yalta Conference –
   a meeting in Crimea between Roosevelt, Churchill, and Stalin
   in February 1945, during which the post World War II division
   and borders of Eastern and Central Europe were agreed upon by
   the Allies.

About the Author

 Myroslaw Kalba was born in Western Ukraine on February 1, 1916, into the family of a prosperous landowner. At the age of eighteen, he joined the Organization of Ukrainian Nationalists (OUN). Having earned a degree from the College of Agronomy in Czernichow, Poland, Kalba returned home to manage his family's farm, which he did until March of 1939, when he was drafted into the Polish Army. He was captured by the Nazis during the German invasion of Poland in September, 1939, and remained a prisoner of war until his release in the spring of 1941.

Upon his release from the German POW camp, he was ordered by his superiors in the OUN to report for duty with the Nachtigall Battalion. After several months, the Battalion was disbanded and its members regrouped into Shutzmannshaftsbattalion-201, until it was dissolved in December, 1942. Kalba was able to return to his family's farm, and during the following summer he married Irena Saluk, a pharmacist.

Early in 1944, Myroslaw Kalba became a training officer in the Ukrainian Insurgent Army (UPA) in the Carpathian Mountains. After a few months, however, he was forced to seek medical treatment for rheumatic fever and could not return to his duties in the UPA. As the Soviet Army advanced into Galicia in the summer of 1944, Kalba fled to Vienna. Soon he was joined by his wife and other members of his family. At the end of the war in May, 1945, the author and his wife entered a Displaced Persons camp in Passau, in American-occupied Bavaria. Their two children were born in the camp. In May, 1949, the family emigrated to the United States and eventually became U.S. citizens.

In the United States, the family first lived on a farm in Iowa. Shortly thereafter they moved to Omaha, Nebraska, until finally settling in Denver, Colorado. Following Irena's death in 1985, the author moved to the Detroit area. In 1999, he married Maria Zembitska.

Kalba always had been active in his local Ukrainian-American communities, seeking to preserve his cultural heritage and to familiarize his fellow Americans with Ukrainian history and traditions. While living in Omaha and Denver, he also was actively involved in American political campaigns on the local, state and national levels.

Myroslaw Kalba wrote six books and many articles dealing with the Nachtigall Battalion and his personal experiences during World War II. He lectured on these topics in the United States, Canada and Ukraine.

Myroslaw Kalba died on January 21, 2013, before his last book was published.

Bibliography

English

Andrew, Christopher and Gordievsky, Oleg. *KGB; The Inside Story.* New York: Harper Collins, 1990. Print.

Andrew, Christopher and Vasili Mitrokhin. *The Sword and the Shield; The Mitrokhin Archive and the Secret History of the KGB.* New York: Basic Books, 1999. Print.

Germany (East) Committee for German Unity. *The Truth about Oberlander; Brown Book on the Criminal Fascist Past of Adenauer's Minister.* Berlin:1960. Print.

Hoffmann, Joachim. *Stalin's War of Extermination 1941-1945; Planning, Realization and Documentation.* Trans. William Deist. Capshaw: Theses Dissertations Press, 2001. Print.

The International Military Tribunal, U.S.S.R. Ex.6RG238. Nurnberg.

Leverkuehn, Paul and R.H. Stevens. *German Military Intelligence.* London: Weidenfeld & Nicolson, 1954. Print.

Mayer, S.L., ed. "The meaning of the struggle; for the freedom and unity of Europe." *Signal: Hitler's Wartime Picture Magazine.* Englewood Cliffs: Prentice-Hall, Inc., 1976. Print.

Raschhofer, Hermann. *Political Assassination; The Legal Background of the Oberlander and Stashinsky Cases.* Tubingen: F. Schlichtenmayer, 1964. Print.

Snyder, Timothy. *Bloodlands; Europe between Hitler and Stalin.* New York: Basic Books, 2010. Print.

Soviet War News – No.1047, December 30, 1944, London: Print.

Sudoplatov, Pavel, et al. *Special Tasks: The Memoirs of an Unwanted Witness - a Sovie Spymaster.* Boston: Little, Brown and Company, 1994. Print.

German

Brockdorff, Werner. *Geheimkommandos des Zweiten Welkrieges* München-Wels:Verlag Welsermühl, 1967. Print.

Ilnyckyj, Roman. *Deutschland und die Ukraine, 1934 - 1945; Tatsachen europaischer Ostpolitik*. 2. Aufl. Munchen: Osteuropa-Institut, 1958. Print.

Polish

Albert, Zygmunt. *Lwowski Wydzial Lekarski w Czasie Okupaciji Hitlerowskej, 1941-1944*. Wroclaw: Zakład Narodowy im. Ossolińskich, 1975. Print.

Bonusiak, Wlodzimierz. *Kto Zabil Professorow Lwowskich*. Rzeszow: Krajowa Agencja Wydawnicza, 1989. Print.

Gerhard, Jan. *Luny w Bieszczadach*. 2vols.Warszawa: 1960. Ministerstwa Obrony Narodowej.

Kalba, Myroslaw. *Nachtigal Ukrainski Batalion 1941*. Detroit-Lviv: Druzyny Ukrainskich Nacionalistiv. 1995. Print.

Korman, Alexander. *Z Krwawych Dni Lwowa, 1941 Roku Krwawy Błekitno-zółty Tydzie Ukraińskiej Irredenty*. London: Koło Lwowian, 1990. Print.

Kultura. Paryz: 1960 (styczen-luty). Print.

Przeglad Lekarski, rok XX, Seria II. Krakow: 1964.(No. 1). Print.

Szczesniak, Anton and Szota, Wieslaw. Wojskowy Instytut Historyczny (Poland). *Droga do Nikad Działalność Organizacji Ukraińskich Nacjonalistów i Jej Likwidacja w Polsce*. Warszawa: Wydawn. Ministerstwa Obrony Narodowej. 1973. Print.

Weliczker, Leon. *Brygada Smierci*: (*Sonderkommando1005*): *Pamiętnik*. Lodz: Centralna Zydowska Komisja Historyczna w Polsce, 1946. Print.

Wojskowy Przeglad Historyczny, Nr. 4. Warszawa: 1988. Print.

Russian

Dmytruk, Klym. *Svastyka na Sutanakh.* Moskva: Izd-vo polit. lit-ry, 1976. Print.

Protocol no. 47. Sasiedaniye Chrezvychayn Gosudarstvennoy Kommissiyi ot 1944 Goda. Print.

Suvorov, Viktor. *Den' - M : Kogda Nacalas' Vtoraja Mirovaja Vojna: Prodolzenie Knigi "Ledokol."* Cherkassy: "Inles," 1994. Print.

Ukrainian

Byelayev, B.P. *Ya Zvynuvachuyu.* Kyiv: 1980. Print.

Bilas, Ivan. *Represyvno-Karalna Systema v Ukraini 1917-1953: Suspilno-Politychnyi ta Istoryko-Pravovyi Analiz: U Dvokh Knyhakh.* Kyiv: Lybid: "Viisko Ukrainy," 1994. Print.

Danylenko, S. T. *Dorohoju Han'by i Zrady : (Istorychna Khronika).* Kyiv: "Naukova dumka," 1970. Print.

Dmytruk, Klym. *Bezbatchenky: Pravda Pro Uchast Ukrainskykh Burzhuaznykh Natsionalistiv i Tserkovnykh Iierarkhiv u Pidhotovtsi Napadu Fashystskoyi Nimechchyny na SRSR.* Lviv: Vyd-vo "Kameniar," 1974. Print.

Haisynovych, Mykhailo Davydovych. *U Zmovi z Katamy.* Lviv: Kameniar, 1975. Print.

Kalba, Myroslaw. *U lavakh Druzhynnykiv: Spohady Uchasnykiw.* Denver: Druzhyn Ukrainskykh Nationalistiv, 1982. Print.

Kalba, Myroslaw. *Nachtigal' Kurin' DUN: u Svitli Factiv i Dokhumentiv.* Denver: Ukrapress, 1984. Print.

Kalba, Myroslaw. *DUN (Druzhyny Ukrainskykh Natsionalistiv).* Detroit: Druzhyn Ukrainskykh Natsionalistiv, 1992. Print.

Kalba, Myroslaw and Oleh Romaniv. *My Prysyahaly Ukrayini: DUN 1941-1943.* Lviv: Naukove t-vo im. Shevchenka, 1999. Print.

Kalba, Myroslaw. *DUN u Rozbudovi UPA. Vydannia Druzhyn Ukrainskykh Natsionalistiv (DUN) (Kureni Nachtigall i Roland).* Detroit-Ternopil: Dzhura, 2005. Print.

Krokhmaliuk, Roman. *Zahrava na Skhodi: Spohady i Dokumenty z Pratsi u Viiskovii Upravi "Halychyna" v 1943-1945 Rokakh.* Toronto: Nakladom Bratstva Kol. Voiakiv Pershoi Ukrainskoi Dyvizii UNA, 1978. Print.

Lebed, Mykola. *UPA, Ukrainska Povstanska Armiia: Yiyi Heneza, Rist i Dii u Vyzvolnii Borotbi Ukrainskoho Narodu za Ukrainsku Samostiinu Sobornu Derzhavu.* [S.l.]: Vydannia Presovoho Biura UGVR, 1946. Print.

Litopys UPA, Vol. 9, Book two, 1946 - 48 with English summaries. Toronto: UPA. 1982. Print.

Maslowsky, Vitaliy. *Zhovto Blakytna Mafiya.* Lviv: Maso, 1975. Print.

Mirchuk, Petro. *Ukrayinska Povstanska Armiya, 1942-1952.* Munich: Cicero, 1953. Print.

Mirchuk Petro. *Roman Shukhevych - Heneral Taras Chuprynka.* London, N.Y: Tovarystvo Kolyshnikh Voiakiv UPA v ZSA, Kanadi i Evropi, 1970. Print.

Pobihushchy-Ren, Yevhen. *Mozayika Moyikh Spomyniv.* Munich: Obiedannia Buvshykh Voiakiv Ukraintsiv u Veelykii Brytanii, 1985. Print.

Stetsko, Yaroslav. *30 chervnya 1941: Proholoshennia Derzhavnosty Ukrainy.* Toronto: Ukrainska Vydavnycha Spilka, 1967. Print.

Suchasnist. Munich: 1983 (January-February). Print.

Ukrayinska Dumka. London: 1978, Nos. 9, 10, 14, 1982, No.5. Print.

Wasylevych, Bohdan. *Lzhemisiya:Pamflety i Narysy (Pro Ukrainskykh Natsionalistiv).*Lviv:Kameniar. 1973. Print.

Wozniak, N. *Yikh Spravzhnye Oblycchya.* Uzhorod: 1974. Print.

Made in the USA
San Bernardino, CA
12 February 2020